75

D0732719

TAXI
Confidential

TAXI
Confidential

Life, Death and 3 a.m. Revelations in New York City Cabs

Amy Braunschweiger

671
Press

First Edition, September 2009

This is a work of nonfiction, and as such, portrays real people and depicts true events. The author changed the name of the some of the characters to preserve their anonymity (and those that were changed are marked with asterisks in the book). The stories in this book came from people's memories. The storytellers interviewed for the book remembered their experiences exactly as they relayed them to the author.

ISBN 0-9821733-2-6
ISBN-13 978-0-9821733-2-9

Book design by Tom Heffron
671 Press logo design by Micah Edel

www.671press.com

Printed in the United States of America

Photography by Amy Braunschweiger and Lee Klancher

For my parents,
who have bravely dealt with my writing habit

Contents

Introduction

Look inside a New York taxicab and you'll see strangers, often from different parts of the world, sitting together in a confined space. Normally, nothing happens: services rendered, money paid.

But sometimes the unexpected—say, a lapdog with bladder issues—enters into the mix. Confronting these types of unpredictable events, whether small or large, can unleash a burst of emotions and scattered actions. Everyone is stuck together in a canary yellow four-door sedan. Unless you throw yourself out the door and into traffic, you have to ride the situation out.

This book focuses on those moments when a variable flies into the equation like a blade, throwing everyone off course and forcing the driver and passenger to interact.

Finding these moments required patience. I spent many hours meeting cabbies at coffee shops, talking with them on cell phones, and riding around in their taxis. There were accents and vocabulary barriers to wade through. The drivers and passengers featured here recreated dialogue from their memory, where they also pulled the scenes' scents and colors. Sometimes they barely tolerated my questions. Many drivers initially denied having any life-changing experiences in their taxis. But we would continue talking about other things, like the new global positioning system or driving in the rain, and gradually, around thirty minutes into the conversation, just as I was about to give up, their memories would loosen. It usually went something like this: "Nope, not much interesting ever happens to me. Never. It's not that great. Well, there was this one time a crackhead dad left his son in my car . . . ."

Learning about drivers' day-to-day existence fascinated me. I always knew they had a tough job, unrelated to the fact that they deal with New York City traffic twelve hours a day. As a former waitress, I've had drunken customers threaten to sue me because they burned their hands on hot plates; others screamed at me when I wouldn't hand out my phone number. I understand how rough it is depending on the public for tips. But after hearing stories of drivers' run-ins with their ungrateful and sometimes crazy passengers, I know they have it worse.

For starters, they work under a perpetual threat of violence. Cabbies carry wads of cash and they're (generally) unarmed. Also they have their back to any passengers. "I feel like a rolling yellow ATM," one cabbie told me. Many drivers I talked to had been robbed more than once, some with guns held to their temples, some with knives to their throats, and one with a piano wire cutting into his neck. Those that haven't been assaulted say things like, "I've been lucky."

Unfortunately, many drivers don't find the police particularly helpful in these situations. The way drivers talk, you'd think cabbies and cops were natural-born adversaries. I didn't hear a single story involving a police officer where the cop came out looking rosy. Logically, it fits. Cabbies spend most of their days driving; many cops spend their days policing the streets. Most drivers grew up in developing countries, living in fear of cops who have something close to carte blanche. Add to this the fact that many drivers are Muslim, don't have U.S. citizenship, and actively fear deportation. At this point, any confrontation with the police becomes terrifying.

Yet it's not potential violence or a perceived unsympathetic police force that weighs heaviest on taxi drivers' minds. Their biggest worry—

the albatross around their necks, the straw breaking the camel's back, the horror that overshadows all others—is where to go to the bathroom.

If you don't spend your waking hours driving a car, this thought probably never crosses your mind. But drivers everywhere know this pain. The big difference is that most drivers can count on highway rest stops. Cabbies, on the other hand, can only count on restrooms in Starbucks and Barnes & Noble, where the staff generally turns a blind eye to non-patrons using their facilities. The same can't be said for the thousands of other restaurants and bars in the city. And there's another catch: before using the restroom, cabbies have to park their taxis. As any New Yorker knows, hunting for a parking space can take thirty minutes and leave you blocks away from your destination. All this leads to the natural conclusion that an entrepreneur should enter the untapped market of "pee bags" for drivers.

Then there's puke. New Yorkers love laughing over their "I puked in a cab" stories. But here's the thing. Drivers have to clean that up themselves. On a bad day, they may not have latex gloves on hand. It could take an hour to wipe up the chunks, then wash and disinfect the backseat. During this hour, the driver is not making any money, despite having already paid more than one hundred dollars up-front for his daily lease. And let's not forget the lingering smell. Following customers won't likely tip well because who wants to ride in a cab with vomit air freshener?

But driving a cab isn't all bad. Cabbies tell many of their stories with an underlying sense of humor and pride, like they sense the lunacy of driving a guy to the hospital only to discover he had a butcher knife sticking out of his back. The greenest cabbie driving nights has experienced far more of the city's raw underside than most New Yorkers.

Unlike a cabbie friend of mine, I have never been in a car with a group of transvestite hookers, all wearing feather boas, slugging back forties, and smoking crack while listening to rap music and watching the sun rise as their taxi barrels into Brooklyn. Another driver I spoke with chuckled while retelling how she overheard a prostitute and her pimp bickering in the back of her cab like a married couple with an unusually colorful vocabulary. Other drivers slap their knee and laugh over stories of tourists, so drunk they can barely walk, asking them to find cheap hookers. Not clean hookers, mind you, just cheap ones. Locals and out-of-town convention attendees alike regularly ask taxi drivers to find them weed or cocaine. If drivers had resumes, they could easily include "pimp" and "drug dealer" under their job description.

Even on the most average night, cabbies see couples making out, or more, in the back seat. On other nights, drivers can expect the offer of sexual favors from willing passengers, both gay and straight.

Sometimes, while listening to a driver's litany of stories, I get jealous. I want to drive a cab, to make exploring the city and meeting its crazy inhabitants my job, to encounter the unexpected and hope for the bizarre.

Then I think about New York's traffic and wonder where I'd go to the bathroom.

CHAPTER 1

SCARED SENSELESS

Fares that Make the Brave Turn Yellow

Many cabbies spend their days contemplating the threat of bodily harm. Not the wrenching-their-back-out-unloading-Louis-Vuitton-luggage bodily harm, but the gun-against-the-temple kind. Drivers work alone, carry socks full of cash and often work nights, making them easy targets. To combat this, cabbies adopted a number of methods to help keep themselves safe.

1. Cab drivers avoid picking up people they think may rob them. This takes skill, because it means being psychic. And while the white guy in the Armani suite may have looted millions from investors, he's not the man cabbies ignore while hailing a cab. The success rate of this particular strategy? Who knows. The legality? Zero—drivers are required to pick up all street hails. People who shout "racism!" because of this practice? Plenty.

2. Cabbies also avoid certain neighborhoods, especially at night. This also requires mind reading, as drivers need to deduct where people hailing cabs live before actually stopping the taxi. The success rate, legality of, and questions of racism stemming from this practice? See number 1.

3. Taxi drivers would never protect themselves by stashing weapons within arms length——that would be illegal. But lots of drivers really like baseball, and keep a sturdy bat handy. Others keep sharp screwdrivers handy, just in case something needs fixing.

4. Some garages and taxi owners install cameras in their cars. This way, after they get robbed they can watch the video and fully appreciate how carefully the perpetrator was masked.

5. Careful drivers don't make multiple stops for the same passenger, because passengers who can't decide on a destination are often looking for the perfect dark corner to rob the driver. Instead, when passengers attempt to change destinations, cabbies piss the potentially armed people off by attempting to eject them from the car.

On other side of the coin, few passengers fear their drivers. For the most part, the only riders afraid of cabbies are the occasional tourists and a small subset of paranoid women with overactive imaginations. But on the off chance your driver is crazy, or even just drunk, be prepared in advance.

1. Does your driver have slurred speech, dilated pupils and a crack pipe in the passenger seat? Either fasten your seat belt or prepare to escape by keeping your hand poised on the door handle, so you can bang open the door and lunge out of the car the moment the driver slows or stops.

2. Think your driver may try to kidnap you? You're probably paranoid. Even if he's not taking the route you requested, he's probably just being belligerent. But just in case, passengers can snap photos of the back of drivers' heads with low-quality camera phones. Sure, the fuzzy photo won't be much help, but it'll make you feel better.

3. Afraid your driver is lost and that you'll die of dehydration in the cab before arriving at your destination? Assess the situation. If you're in Manhattan and he can't find Sixth Street, he's not a real cabbie. He probably borrowed his cousin's cab and hack license to make a few extra bucks. This probably makes for interesting conversation, so after you give him specific directions, ask him about himself. If you are lost in Brooklyn, just give up. You're never getting out.

4. Is your driver relentlessly hitting on you in a creepy way? First, stop making eye contact. And by all means, don't tell him where you live. Instead, have the driver paramour drop you off a few blocks from your apartment, preferably on a one-way street. Walk in the opposite direction of the cab. Once he peels out of sight, double back to your home.

5. Is your driver giving you hostile looks via the rearview mirror and shaking his fist at you? Get out of the cab. Now. Even if it's moving, get out. Well, not on a highway, but the minute you get on a slower paced side street. When making a break for it, toss some money through the partition, just in case he's willing to pull the cab to a stop, chase you down and pummel you for not paying.

THE CABBIE, THE KID, AND THE CRACKHEAD

~

Peter Caine says that driving a cab is the perfect job for an alcoholic. You can drive a few days straight and fill your pockets with cash, then park the taxi and spend the next few days blowing money on cheap beer and vodka.

That's what he did. He refused to drink and drive. If he got caught, he'd have his license suspended, he'd lose his drinking income and have to get a real job.

Peter started drinking hard when he was fifteen-and-a-half-years-old. Maybe his problems with alcohol were genetic—his mother was part Choctaw and his father was Cherokee, although he told people he was Irish. Peter looked like a white man with dark hair and eyes. Whatever the cause, alcohol posed a problem. Despite his small stature, he would polish off a case of beer and some vodka each night.

His strategy for making money as a New York cabbie was the same one he used while driving a taxi in his hometown of St. Louis. He went to bad neighborhoods that most drivers avoided.

"When I look back on it as a sober person, I was out of my mind," he said. "I think I had a death wish or something."

He drove through "war zones" littered with trash, graffiti and broken windows. At least once a night a customer scared him so badly that he thought, this is it, this one is going to kill me.

Peter had a radio in his cab, and one day he got a call to go to 106th Street on the east side, Spanish Harlem. It was a round-trip call.

Peter knew what that meant—a drug run. It also meant that person was in bad shape. In New York City, drugs—like Kung Pao chicken and egg rolls—are delivered. If someone needs to go out and hunt down drugs, it indicates that their source is ignoring them; one way or another, that person is already in trouble.

Peter drove to the address, and a father and his small son came out of the house and got into the back of the cab. The kid was adorable. He looked like a closer-cropped Rodney Allen Rippey, the little boy in the Jack In The Box commercials. It was the dead of winter, and he wore a fuzzy, red ski hat and red mittens.

They got in the car, and the father gave an address only a few blocks away. Walking distance. The man talked to the child like he cared about him. "We'll do that when we get home, but first Dad's gotta go pick something up," he said.

Peter pulled up to the address. The windows were boarded up, and the place was thick in graffiti. The steps were crumbled and broken glass glittered on the ground. It looked like a crack house. The dad hopped out of the cab, leaving his son behind.

"I'll be right back," he said to both the boy and Peter, before heading to the house.

The kid sat in the back staring straight ahead. He looked scared.

Shit, Peter thought. Who leaves their kid alone with a stranger? He tried to make the kid feel comfortable.

"Hey, how are you?" he asked.

The boy didn't answer.

"Don't worry, your dad will be back here soon."

They waited ten or fifteen minutes, and Peter started to worry. The dad hadn't returned. The kid still hadn't responded to what Peter hoped was comforting chit-chat. He only stared straight ahead. His little body looked tense. Peter didn't know what was going on in the father's head. He didn't know the kid's family. Maybe they were looking for a lawsuit. Maybe they would accuse him of molesting their son.

"Don't worry, your dad will be back soon," he told the kid again, reassuring him.

He dialed his dispatcher.

"I got this little kid in the car," he said. "This fucker went upstairs, he left his kid in the car. What do I do?"

"Hang on 208," the dispatcher said.

He stayed on the line with the dispatcher, giving himself an alibi in case the father tried to accuse him of anything.

He turned around to the boy again. The child's face was serious.

He knew what was going on. It was sad. Poor kid, Peter thought. He doesn't deserve this. Peter's own father was an alcoholic, and he knew how it was.

"How old are you?" he asked.

The kid stayed silent.

"Four?"

Nothing.

"Five?"

The kid nodded his head up and down, looking straight ahead.

Peter had seen some bad things as a driver—once someone tried to kill him by wrapping a wire around his throat; another time someone held a steak knife to his neck and robbed him—but this was a new type of terror. He should have stuck to his original plan and become a dog walker, he thought, or maybe he could be a bike messenger again.

But driving had its advantages. For one, while he drove around he looked for junk on the street to make art. Found objects, he called them. He created a solid name for himself in the St. Louis art scene this way. He was doing the same thing in New York. He built ensembles of often life-sized animated figures, programming them to perform angry and grotesque physical acts involving sex or bodily functions. Almost all his work ultimately commented on politics, religion, or both, like in "Every Cop's Fantasy," where the scene contained a black man—more 3D cartoon image than real person with his red mouth and bulging eyes. His pants hung around his ankles, while a bald, white cop wearing aviator sunglasses assaulted him.

Critics called his work perverse, but nothing he built could top a father leaving his kid alone in a cab.

It was almost half an hour since the dad had disappeared.

Peter noticed the baseball insignia on the boy's jacket.

"You like baseball?" he asked.

The boy nodded yes.

"You have a favorite team?"

No answer. Peter talked a bit about baseball. He couldn't believe the dad left his son with a stranger.

"We'll stay here until your dad gets back," he said.

He hoped the father would come back. He was sitting there, with the meter on, for more than half an hour. Let this guy not be too fucked up to walk out of that house, Peter thought.

The front door of the house opened, and the dad came out. He got into the back of the cab as if nothing were wrong, as if his absence were no big deal. He didn't seem paranoid like other people who smoked crack in Peter's cab. But at that point Peter was so mad he didn't care. The dad was an asshole. Peter wanted to yell at the guy, but held himself in check for the kid's sake.

Peter drove them the few blocks home. "That'll be thirty-two dollars," he said.

"Listen, I don't have any money," the father replied.

Peter glared at him.

The father took the red mittens and hat off his kid. The boy's face was sad; he looked at the ground.

"Here, take these," the dad said, handing the mittens and hat to Peter.

Peter wanted to scream, but he didn't want to upset the kid. He took the ease with which the father handed over the kid's hat and gloves as a sign he had done it before. The dad knew no one in their right mind would ever take those away from a child in the winter.

The dad opened the door for his son, and the boy got out.

While the kid was out of hearing range, Peter leaned back and seethed, "Man, are you fucking nuts? You got that cute little kid! What the fuck is your problem?"

The dad ignored him.

"Keep your kid's gloves and go get some help."

The father and son walked to their door. Peter drove away, shaken. He got on the radio and told his dispatcher about the hat and mittens. He had to tell someone.

MURPHY'S LAW

~

Starving actor Davidson Garrett was a terrible waiter and could barely cover his rent. He needed a survival job; something to bring in cash while he acted in off-off Broadway shows. In 1978, he settled on driving a cab—something lots of writers and actors did to support their passions.

This was back when cabbies made more money, splitting their cash take with the garages. This was before the implementation of the current leasing system—or sweatshop system, as Davidson calls it—where cabbies pay garages a flat fee regardless of the dollars they bring in. In the good old days when the city deemed extensive course work and drug testing an unnecessary nuisance, scoring a hack license was simple. Davidson got his license in three days, and it only put him back fifteen dollars. The one-page test posed questions like, "Where's the Empire State Building?"

As a new driver, Davidson was low man on the totem pole of two hundred drivers working at his greasy, exhaust-filled garage at Eighteenth Street and Tenth Avenue. Mechanics swarmed the place, maintaining and repairing the garage's one hundred taxis. The cabs were divvied out to drivers by the garage's dispatcher, a short, fat, tightly-wound Puerto Rican who chain-smoked and enjoyed screaming. He was a real-life incarnation of Danny Devito's character on *Taxi*.

Davidson was a new driver—a nobody. The garage saw driver turnover of about 20 percent each week, and he knew the dispatcher would never distinguish his face from the hundreds of others. The dispatcher also liked to pull power plays on drivers. Sometimes he would make drivers sit for an hour waiting for a taxi, even through the garage was filled with cabs, just to remind them who was boss.

To the dispatcher, Davidson was a hack, not a human being.

But like every other driver in the garage, he kept trying to gain the dispatcher's favor by greasing the guy's palm with a few dollars before every shift. He saw how it worked. The more some drivers tipped, the nicer the dispatcher treated them. Davidson was just waiting for his good garage karma to kick in. In the meantime, the dispatcher inevitably gave him taxis with worn-out shocks, dented hoods and doors, and an ungodly number of miles on the engine. Customers complained about the funky-smelling upholstery.

Davidson had worked the garage for about a year when the dispatcher asked him, "Can you handle a brand-new taxi?"

The angels sang. The earth moved. Davidson had ascended into the highest regions of taxi culture. The dispatcher actually remembered who he was! He had been a faithful driver with no accidents, and he had consistently tipped generously, and it was finally paying off.

"Yes," Davidson said.

He was thrilled. The gleaming cab had literally come off the assembly line the week before; it still had the $27,000 ticket price on the window. He got into the cab and ran his hand over the seat's shiny upholstery and inhaled the new car smell. It was his first time driving a brand-new car. His settled into the firm and comfortable seat, knowing it would be good for his back. He turned the key, and the engine purred. The muffler was silent. Almost as soon as he left the garage, Davidson hit a pothole. But there was no jarring sensation in his spine, and the supple suspension silently absorbed the bump rather than groaning and knocking in protest. He smiled. Customers would love the smooth, quiet ride, and he hoped they would tip accordingly.

It was 3:30 in the morning when Davidson drove up Lexington near Twenty-eighth Street, an area known for prostitutes. He was sitting at a red light when three overweight white women came running towards his cab and jumped in the backseat.

"Mister, step on it! Step on it!" they yelled.

He craned his neck towards the back seat, taking in the women's tight mini dresses, heavy mascara and the feather boas wrapped around their necks. They were clearly working girls.

He weighed his words carefully. "I'm at a red light, and I'll wait until the light changes."

"Mister you better get going!" one of them warned.

"I can't step on it. I've got a brand-new cab, there's a red light, and I have to be very careful."

At that moment, an angry young man appeared before his cab, brandishing a crowbar. Hostile intent pinched his face and he took a confrontational stance. He shook the crowbar in front of the taxi.

"Give me back my wallet!" he yelled.

Davidson froze with terror. Both his hands seemed stuck to the wheel. This guy is going to kill me, he thought. The women in the backseat screamed at the top of their lungs. Davidson wanted to push the gas pedal, but couldn't—he'd run over the Jersey-looking brute and go to jail. He never thought to put the car in reverse and gun it. Davidson had heard of cabbies being killed left and right. This was going to be his moment. He imagined the next day's front-page headline, "Cabbie Killed by Crowbar." The women screamed like Fay Wray in *King Kong*.

In a quick, fluid motion, the man brought the crowbar down on Davidson's windshield. The glass smashed. Then he ran round the right side of the car to the rear door. The women hollered, and squished each other moving to the left side of the car. He could hear them trying to get out. They couldn't. They must have locked the doors when they saw the man. Davidson still couldn't move.

The man raised the crowbar and slammed it into the window. The glass smashed. Shards fell onto the backseat. The girls screamed their heads off. The man reached into the cab and slapped the nearest woman and pawed at the others. His full torso was almost in the car. He grabbed the closest woman's hair, and yanked her towards the window. He yelled and pulled harder, dragging her across the shards of grass. He tried to force her through the broken window. Davidson watched the scene unfold like something out of a film noir movie, with the girls screaming bloody murder and the guy beating everyone he could reach.

One of the women finally managed to unlock her door. She bounded out of the cab, followed by the other two, feather boas flying behind them as they trundled up the street. The john chased them up Lexington Avenue, brandishing his crowbar.

Davidson was left sitting alone in his brand-new cab, which was now covered with shattered glass from the broken windshield and back window. He had never experienced the truly dark side of taxi driving before, although later he would publish his adventures in his book of cabbie poetry, *King Lear of the Taxi*. Davidson collected himself, pulled over to the nearest pay phone, and dialed 911. It took forty-five minutes for the cops to show. But Davidson waited, as he needed a police report before going back to the garage and facing the dispatcher. He needed to prove that the busted cab wasn't his fault.

He figured it would be a while before he picked up hookers.

After the police left, Davidson drove back to the garage. When he pulled in, the dispatcher's jaw dropped when he saw the beautiful new car limping in with a shattered windshield and missing window. The dispatcher ran out from his Plexiglas-windowed office.

"What happened! What happened! I thought you could handle a new cab!"

A KIDNAPPING IN QUEENS

~

Melissa Garba and her friend, Kathleen, were going abroad for the first time to study in Spain. But instead of flying directly from their home state of Ohio to Queen's Kennedy airport, where their flight to Spain originated, they decided to look for a cheaper deal. They found one to Long Island's Islip airport. It would require they take a fifteen-dollar shuttle to Kennedy, but it would ultimately save them one hundred dollars each. Besides, Queens couldn't be that far—the Web site did bill Islip as a New York City airport, after all.

The trip to Islip went smoothly. After landing, someone manning the information desk called the shuttle service, as both girls had left their cell phones at home. It was a cold, January afternoon, and the usual gray cloud covering New York during the winter had disappeared, in its place a rare blue sky. Melissa wore her silver puffy coat, and the pair waited outside for their ride on a black metal bench.

Their shuttle pulled up, looking like any other van—white, with the name of the company splayed across the side. The driver, a lanky, African man, seemed nice enough, and helped Melissa foist her massive duffle bag into the vehicle.

The girls were the only two passengers in the van, and they took the back seat right behind the driver. It felt like their own private shuttle. The driver pulled out, and they were barely under way when his cell phone rang. He took the call, speaking in a foreign language. A minute after he hung up he got another call. More calls came in rapid succession. With each call, the driver became more agitated, yelling into his phone.

"Did you hear what he just said in English?" Kathleen whispered to Melissa.

"No, what?" Melissa said back.

"He said he needs to bail his brother out of jail!" she said, panicked.

Melissa looked at her.

"I swear!" Kathleen hissed. "Should we ask him?"

"No!" was Melissa's definitive reply.

Growing concerned about their driver's volatile mood, the girls glanced out the window. They had no idea where they were. Neither had visited New York before, and neither knew how to reach Kennedy, but both assumed they should be on some kind of major highway. Instead, the driver was cruising down side streets. The neighborhoods became sketchier and sketchier. They exchanged looks.

TAXIS, CAR SERVICES AND GYPSY CABS

~

When it comes to driving around New Yorkers, yellow cabs are the sexy, high-profile choice. But most people also use the red-headed stepsisters of the yellow cab; car services and gypsy cabs.

Manhattan is the official lair of the yellow cab, whose drivers stop for street hails and try at all costs to avoid the outer boroughs. Up until the 1980s, yellow cabs also received radio calls to pick up passengers, but today, radio calls are the realm of the car service.

Because yellow cabs are hard to come by in Brooklyn and Queens, the Taxi and Limousine Commission (TLC) charges car services with picking up the slack in these areas. Outer borough people who need a ride call the car service, and the black cars pick them up from their homes. It is illegal for car service drivers to stop for street hails.

True gypsy cabs are illegal, unregulated and harder to spot, unless you're at an airport luggage carousel, where a dozen drivers clamor, "Need a ride? Need a ride?" Oftentimes, riding in a gypsy cab is like sitting in some dude's car, complete with torn seats and food smells. For the right price, gypsy cabs— and car services— go into neighborhoods where yellow cabs are too, well, yellow to go. Because of this, gypsy cab drivers are more frequent victims of violent crimes than those who drive their canary yellow cousins.

The driver finally got off the phone. He turned to the girls.

"I need all your money right now," he said. "I need to pay parking tickets."

Melissa stared at him.

"We don't have a lot of money," Melissa told him, glancing sideways at Kathleen. "We would prefer to just pay our fifteen dollars."

The driver looked flustered and agitated.

"I need to pay these tickets!" he barked. "Give me your money!"

"Well, we'd …" Melissa began before the cabbie cut her off.

"Then I won't take you to the airport," he shouted. "I need that money!"

Kathleen reached into her bag. Melissa followed suit. Between the two of them, they cobbled together one hundred dollars in twenty-dollar bills. Melissa hoped the driver wouldn't find the travel packs fastened around their waists under their coats, where they both hid hundreds of dollars in traveler's checks. They handed him the cash, which he placed on his lap.

They arrived at the precinct.

"Where are we?" Kathleen asked.

"Queens," the driver answered. He put the money in his pocket. "I will return in a few minutes," he said.

He got out of the van and locked the doors behind him.

Terrified, Melissa turned to Kathleen. "Oh God, do we run? Do we try and get a taxi? What do we do?"

"Let's make a run for it," Kathleen said.

First, Melissa tried the van's sliding side door, but it was broken. They couldn't get out.

"Not only did he take our money, but he's kidnapping us," Melissa whispered.

She wanted to get the hell out of the van.

In their panic, they didn't think to try the front doors. They also never thought to walk into the precinct and tell the cops what happened. The two sat there for about ten minutes, hashing out strategies to run, get a taxi or even stay in the van. The more they looked out the window, the more the surrounding area scared them. Bands of men—drug dealers?—loitered on the street along with roving groups of kids who should have been in school. The situation could be as bad outside of the van as inside of it.

"We're screwed," Kathleen said.

Ugly images flitted through their minds—would the man drive off with them? Would they ever reach the airport? She never had the impression the driver would hurt them, but knew anything could happen.

"Why the hell were we so cheap?" Melissa cried. "Are we really worth only one hundred dollars?"

Melissa saw the van's CB radio dangling. She stretched her five-foot frame forward and grabbed the device. She radioed for help. Someone answered, but the connection was bad and everything sounded garbled. Then she looked out the window and saw the driver coming out of the precinct doors. She dropped the CB and sat back in her seat.

He unlocked the doors and climbed back in, saying nothing. He put the key into the ignition, turned it and started the van. He mumbled something about parking tickets under his breath.

"Listen, we need to get to the airport," Melissa said. "We really need to make this flight. Please?"

She wondered why the driver needed so little money to pay his parking tickets. Surely they totaled much more! And why did he walk back to the van alone if he needed to bail out his brother? What had he done with their money?

She glanced at Kathleen, who was trying to persuade the driver to take them to the airport.

The driver's cell phone started ringing. He took the call, yelling. As he yelled, his driving became erratic. He braked hard at stop signs, then slammed the accelerator. He barely slowed before peeling around corners and hardly seemed to check for oncoming traffic before turning. The girls felt nauseous.

"Should we throw ourselves out the door?" Melissa quietly asked Kathleen, who shook her head no.

Melissa was pretty sure they might not make it. What were they thinking buying those cheap tickets?

They continued passing through crowded neighborhoods peppered with abandoned industrial buildings and graffiti-covered walls. Groups of men sat on stoops near the street.

Melissa crossed her fingers in hopes they'd actually reach Kennedy. Amazingly, half an hour later they did just that. The driver even stopped the van at the appropriate terminal.

"It's a miracle!" Kathleen said.

They girls hauled their luggage from the van. Melissa took a deep breath and faced the driver. "We'd like our one hundred dollars back."

"I have no idea what you're talking about," he said.

"The one hundred dollars you stole from us!" Kathleen yelled.

"I have no idea what you mean," he answered. "That will be fifteen dollars each," he said. Kathleen gaped at him.

"We don't have any money!" Melissa screamed. "You took it all!" The driver pretended not to understand.

They grabbed their luggage, rushed inside and checked their bags. When they met up with the group of students they were studying abroad with, they told their story. No one believed them. Melissa went to the pay phone and called her parents, shocking them with the tale. Then she called the shuttle service and asked to speak with a manager.

"I'm not responsible for the route each driver took," the manager told Melissa. "As long as you made it to you destination in time, they did their job."

"I want my money back," Melissa argued. Barely a consolation, two months later her father received a refund check for fifteen dollars.

Despite being robbed and kidnapped her first time in the Big Apple, Melissa moved to New York after finishing college and serving in the Peace Corps. And after living in New York, she realized the areas of Queens they drove through were more decent than frightening. But while she didn't blame the city for her experience, the borough of Queens brings a bad taste to her mouth.

"I swear I will never live in Queens," she says. "I've been there, I've visited friends there, but I will never move there."

Nor will she ever fly out of Islip—even if the tickets are priced rock bottom.

KNOCKOUT

~

Tim Zino was running towards Penn Station. He had five minutes before hopping on a train to Long Island, where he would meet with his ex-girlfriend. Tim took out his cell phone, looked at the time, snapped the phone shut and stepped off the curb at Thirty-seventh Street and Seventh Avenue. The next thing he knew he was on the hood of a cab.

"Son of a bitch," he muttered, getting off the cab.

Tim gave the driver an angry look and, being a New Yorker, punched the hood of his cab.

The cabbie took his foot off the brake and hit Tim again with his taxi.

Pissed off, Tim pounded the hood of the cab twice more with his fist and walked to the driver's door. He wanted to talk to this son of a bitch, get in his face a bit and ask him what his problem was.

The driver threw open the door, purposely pushing it into Tim. The cabbie started getting out of the cab. Pissed off because the driver just hit him twice then deigned to hit him again with a door, Tim reacted. He slammed the cab door on the driver's head.

The driver yelled out. He shoved the door open, stepped out, and took a swing at Tim. Tim moved out of the way, ducking the driver's fist by inches.

Then Tim's stomach dropped.

The driver was huge. He was well over six feet tall and looked like he'd weigh in at 270 pounds. He was a beast. Compared to him, Tim was a featherweight, at five-foot-seven weighing less than 150, including his suit and overcoat.

The driver came at Tim sideways, like a boxer.

Oh fuck, Tim thought. His mind went into high gear, trying to figure out how to avoid getting his ass kicked. The driver was barreling at him. Tim went for his knees.

The big dude swung at him again, putting all his weight into the punch. Tim moved to the left, drew back his fist and nailed the driver in the nose.

The guy took a step back, and refocused on Tim with renewed energy. The fight was on.

The driver's punch slammed into Tim's face, and he fell to the ground. Tim dodged the guy's feet and got back up. Adrenaline rushed through his body.

The two exchanged a series of blows, Tim's speed and scrappiness helped him dodge his opponent's flying fists. But the punches that hit him hurt. Tim managed to land a number of punches on the guy. Both lost their balance and hit the ground a few times. Tim doesn't understand why they guy didn't pummel him—he figures he was lucky, that the adrenaline kept him spot on. Whatever it was, they were somehow at a draw.

Then Tim slugged the driver in the face. The guy stumbled backwards, hit the curb, fell into Seventh Avenue and almost got run over by a bus.

The driver got up from the street, his glare searing into Tim. Tim was terrified. His stomach jumped to his throat. A guy sitting on a folding chair selling newspapers scampered out of their way.

The driver grabbed the folding chair and lunged at Tim, holding the chair over his head like a weapon. Tim, terrified of the pain, turned around, showing the driver his back. He put his hands over his head. The driver wailed the metal chair across Tim's back. Time slowed down. Everything was in slow-motion. The pounding with the chair didn't seem to hurt. As the driver hit him, it seemed to Tim that the chair lingered on his back. He took his hands off his head, reached over his left shoulder, and grabbed the chair and wrenched it out of the driver's hands.

He spun around and wailed the driver's knees with the chair before throwing the chair down the street.

The driver rushed Tim, Tim pushed him, and out of nowhere, a lady grabbed Tim by his overcoat.

"You gotta stop this, you're scaring us!" she said.

"Scaring you, lady!" Tim retorted. "Are you fucking kidding me?"

Thanks to the woman's interruption, reality set in. For the first time, Tim realized that a swarm of sixty or so people stood in a circle around him, watching the whole thing. People were wrapped around the corner, trying to either see or get past them.

The driver took advantage of Tim's momentary distraction and made for his cab. He got in and took off.

Tim ran down the street after him and took down his license plate. He took out his cell phone and called 911. Tim walked back to the fight scene, but by this point the crowd had dispersed.

The operator told him they'd send someone right away. He waited what seemed like ten or fifteen minutes—but it could have been two minutes—before calling 911 again.

"Hey, you guys going to send somebody over?"

It seemed like the first time in his life he was standing at a corner with no cops around.

Then a GMC Jimmy pulled up and six cops got out. His body hurt, but Tim couldn't help laughing. It was like a clown car, they just didn't stop coming. A couple of the cops chased the cab. Two questioned Tim, but they seemed new on the job. They kept calling their boss and asking what to do.

The ambulance came.

"Hey man, do you mind if I sit down in the back of the ambulance?" Tim asked.

The adrenaline had left his system, and he suddenly felt exhausted. His body had started to hurt.

"We're actually going to put you in the ambulance," an EMT said.

They strapped him in and took him to the hospital.

He sat in the hospital for hours. He called his ex-girlfriend to let her know that he couldn't meet up and that he was in the hospital, but she didn't seem too worried. She was at an Islanders game. He took a cigarette break while waiting for treatment. His body began hurting badly. He smoked a few more cigarettes.

It was nine hours before the hospital released him at 3:30 a.m. By that time, he couldn't bend his leg and he couldn't turn his head. Two of his fingers were swollen as big as lollipops. The doctors told him to take Ibuprofen. His body hurt so badly that his father had to slide him into the car. He was miserable.

The next day, Tim planned on seeing a specialist for his knee and fingers—he played piano and needed to make sure his fingers heeled correctly. But there was a problem. No one would accept his insurance. Because he was hit by a cab, Tim's insurance refused to cover it—Tim needed the taxi garage's insurance. However, the garage hadn't given the correct insurance information. The situation continued for three days, with Tim seeking treatment and insurance companies not coughing up.

He went back to the hospital to talk to them. There, he discovered that his release papers never mentioned an assault and his specific injuries were undocumented. He called the cops, but they had failed to file a police report.

Tim called his lawyer.

His lawyer sued everyone.

Tim was supposed to move to Florida two days after the beating, but that was delayed by three to four weeks. He never did get in to see a doctor, and it took three months for him to play piano without a pain shooting up his arm to his spine. He settled out of court with the cab company and the cab insurance company.

All healed, Tim now makes a living playing piano at a dueling piano bar. He enjoys the comedy aspect of it and the laid-back tiki vibe. It sure beats wrangling with cabbies.

PREGNANCY SCARE

~

Marisol Rodriguez* sat in the back of a cab beside her good friend's sister, Elizabeth, who was visiting from the Dominican Republic. The two spent the warm March afternoon exploring a museum. Marisol, who came to the United States from Puerto Rico years before, placed a hand on her expanded belly as the two women relaxed in the back seat and watched the sun set. She was five months pregnant with her first child. Marisol was constantly hungry, and she looked forward to eating Chinese food when they got home. The driver had annoyed her by insisting on taking a different route than she suggested, but it wasn't a big deal, and it wasn't worth a fight.

Their taxi rushed downtown, passing through Midtown. As they neared Twenty-eighth Street, Marisol saw the light at the intersection turn red to green. Their driver obliviously sped into the intersection, never anticipating someone may run the freshly turned red light adjacent to them. Marisol, who sat behind the passenger's seat, saw the other taxi hurtling towards them. In a split second, she realized the two taxis were going to crash.

Neither she nor Elizabeth wore a seat belt—a common practice for New Yorkers who feel safe knowing they won't be thrown through the windshield from the back of a cab. In those scarce moments before impact, she shielded her stomach by putting up her legs in front of her and sticking her arms straight out. Her driver slammed on his brakes to avoid hitting the other cab, but he didn't react quickly enough. They smashed into the other vehicle with a great crunching sound followed by the tinkling of broken glass.

Upon impact, the women flew forward. Marisol's face slammed into the partition and her head rag-dolled back and forth. Then all went quiet and her world slipped into a vacuum of stillness. Marisol couldn't

---

*Note that names which appear with asterisks next to them have been changed at the request of the storyteller.

think. She sat in the backseat, trying to figure out what happened. Blood poured down her face, but her mind hadn't yet caught up with her circumstances. She couldn't feel her body. She felt disoriented and foggy. It occurred to her that she could be dying.

The cab driver turned to them. "Get out of the cab and give me ten bucks," he said.

Neither woman responded.

Elizabeth slowly opened her door and Marisol followed suit. They stepped out of the cab. They stood outside, looking at the taxis blocking the intersection—both yellow cabs looked seriously dented, but neither was mangled or totaled.

"My back hurts," Elizabeth said. She was sitting behind the driver, and his head had blocked her view of the impending impact. The accident caught her fully unawares.

Marisol tried to walk, but couldn't make her legs work. In fact, she couldn't feel her legs. Her mind was thick and hazy.

The wail of a siren pierced her brain as an ambulance arrived on the scene. A member of the EMS team approached Marisol. He took her blood pressure. It was dropping, he said, one of the body's defense mechanisms when dealing with pain. She was in shock. Marisol felt woozy, like she was drugged. She faintly noticed that a cop spoke with the cab driver, who never got out of the car.

"You should go to the hospital," the EMS worker told her.

"No," Marisol answered. "I want to go home." Home sounded nice and secure. She could go to bed there.

Elizabeth urged her friend to go to the hospital.

Marisol didn't want to be a diva—she prided herself on her independence—but she relented. She was confused and disoriented. Her neck hurt. She felt lightheaded, like she was about to faint.

Once inside the ambulance, she was glad she made the decision to go. She felt safer. Once at the hospital, the doctors checked her over. After the examination, they said her baby would be fine, but Marisol still worried. "What if they don't know?" she thought. The first ten weeks of her pregnancy had already been fretful and difficult. She had bled, and she had worried that she could lose the baby. But after ten weeks, the bleeding stopped. Now, those fears came rushing back.

She wanted to know for sure, but the doctors wouldn't X-ray her because the procedure could harm her baby. They reiterated that she was fine, outside of a broken nose. Elizabeth, who had already passed the doctors' inspection, stayed by her side. "I feel like I've brought you bad luck while you're pregnant!" she said with remorse, herself the mother of five children. "I feel terrible."

Fender Benders

~

Cabbies have a well-deserved reputation of careening through traffic, cutting off semis, and squeaking under yellow lights. Driving antics make for animated water-cooler conversation, with some tales making their way to urban myth status. But for all the complaints that drivers treat the city's sidewalks like side streets, statistics show that New York City's taxi and livery drivers—especially those employed for many years—are the safest drivers in all five boroughs.

For those familiar with New Yorkers' penchants for veering across four lanes of traffic or pulling U-turns on busy streets, this statistic gives little comfort. But that's not the point.

Bruce Schaller of Schaller Consulting undertook the study of accident rates per miles driven, concluding that the city's cabs are involved in 30 percent fewer crashes than all other vehicles. For every million miles driven, cabs had only 4.6 crashes, compared with 6.7 for normal vehicles. Livery drivers were even safer at 3.7 accidents. The reason for this lies in many factors—driver training, economic penalties, time on the road, etc.

That said, taxi passengers are twice as likely to suffer injuries when involved in an accident. Why? Because backseat passengers scoff at seat belts, and if the cab stops suddenly, they fly into the partition—nose first.

Marisol's husband rushed to the hospital when Elizabeth called him. Both he and Elizabeth tried to cheer her up by joking with her and having fun in the hospital. But she couldn't help but worry about the baby. After a little while, Marisol relented to their attempts to cheer her up. She knew she had no control over the situation, over the fact that her face hurt and the fact that she was stuck in the hospital. She smiled, although it hurt, and the three of them joked and had fun until the doctor said she could leave.

The gut-wrenching pain started the next day. "I felt like somebody took me and beat me with a bat," she said. Her whole body was covered in black and blue bruises. Every muscle in her body seemed to scream in agony, rendering her immobile. She couldn't lift her arms to dress herself. She couldn't roll over, put her feet on the floor and physically get out of bed. Normally, she went regularly to yoga classes and lifted weights. Today, she couldn't move. The throbbing from her broken nose spread across her face. If a blanket brushed her cheek while she dozed, the ensuing jolt of pain woke her up.

She called her family doctor, whom she trusted. He couldn't tell her when her body would heal, but he assured her she wouldn't lose the baby. She felt zero pain in her stomach, and she hadn't bled, so she trusted her doctor. But now that worries about her baby's health were allayed, her fear flowed in a new direction. What if her injuries were permanent, but the doctors didn't know? What if she never got better? She thought about the child she carried. Would she be able to care for her baby after she was born? Would she be able to hold her? Marisol couldn't feed or dress herself, how would she be able to feed and dress her baby? Immobile and lost in her dark thoughts, she sank into a deep depression.

It was only the second week after the accident, when she felt marginally better, that she started to think about suing. Her friends brought up the subject.

At first, Marisol didn't want to sue. Then came the problems with her insurance company. Doctors and hospitals didn't want to accept her insurance when she told them she had been in the accident. They knew collecting money from her insurance company would be harder than pulling a hungry lion's teeth. They knew her insurance provider would insist that the cab company was responsible for Marisol's bills.

Not that Marisol was happy with her doctors. An acute pain shot through her back any time she touched it, and her neck ached. If she slept wrong, she'd get a headache. The doctors assumed she had a slipped disk, but couldn't know for sure without taking X-rays—something that would hurt her baby girl. They tried to figure out the problem by pushing Marisol's head down, which resulted in a wave of pain surging through her skull. They decided to put her on meds, but it barely touched the pain.

When it became more difficult for her to get doctors to see her, she began calling lawyers. She needed to make sure someone took care of her medical bills. But she wasn't sure what a lawsuit required, or how much time and energy it would take. But she was angry, depressed, and felt backed into a corner.

Plus, she wasn't able to work. Marisol had invented a medical device, and had planned to start clinical trials for her device that week. But thanks to the accident, she couldn't even write or get out of bed, let alone introduce doctors to her invention, and help analyze data from the device. She also managed a building that she and her husband owned, and repairs needed by her tenants piled up.

Marisol found a lawyer she liked. She decided to sue. Her lawyer suggested suing both cab companies, not just the company of the cab that hit hers. His theory: the other cab—the one that ran the red light—was obviously at fault. But so was her cab driver. First off, he was speeding, and second, he should have practiced defensive driving skills. The most dangerous time to enter an intersection is when the light changes from red to green. He should have watched for people running the red light. Marisol took her lawyer's advice and sued them both.

It was a two-year process. She documented her medical problems and fought the insurance companies that refused to pay for her treatments. Marisol let her lawyer handle the cab companies—she had bigger things on her mind. Like her daughter. A few months into the lawsuit, Marisol had a healthy baby girl, named Esperanza. Seven or eight months after Esperanza was born, Marisol faced her fears and began taking cabs again.

Esperanza was nearly two years old—a smiling girl with black, wavy hair toddling around her parents' place—when both cab companies settled. Marisol was happy with the outcome. She was relieved that someone was finally responsible for her medical bills, although she didn't sue solely for the money. "I was really doing it out of principle," she said. "Somebody runs a light and it can change your life drastically."

CHAPTER 2

WELCOME TO THE NUTHOUSE

Insane Passengers, Bizarre Coincidences,
and Hilarious Experiences

In New York, bizarre occurrences become a part of daily life. Maybe it's the drugs, or perhaps pollution addles the brain. In part, the city's accepting, permissible nature seems to encourage its inhabitants to push boundaries. In any case, I've never before lived somewhere where a businessman let me see the purple bra he wore under his suit, or where a homeless person tried to give me a dead bird.

Whenever something seriously odd occurs in a taxi, the close quarters intensify the experience. If you encounter a ranting man brandishing a crowbar on the street, you give him a wide berth or simply run away. But if the same ranting man drove your cab, you're trapped. Your primary option is to cower near the door and hope for a red light.

In the same vein, see that guy eating with his feet in Tompkins Square Park? How unique. See that guy steering a cab with his feet? Horrifying.

Most experiences, though, are more quirky or interesting than terrifying.

Like coincidences. For a city teeming with eight million people, running into a friend on the sidewalk seems surprisingly easy. The taxi equivalent: A driver picking up the same passenger twice in one day. With 13,000-some cabs, the odds of this are . . . well, let's just say extremely low. Maybe not the type of odds to make Stephen Hawking believe in God, but still. One cabbie believes fate influences these types of coincidences. Another driver told me of the time he picked up the same attractive woman twice in one day. He told her that if he picked her up a third time, they had to marry. She laughed politely, clearly no believer in fate.

And, of course, you have the crazy people.

They can be hard to identify. Because anything goes in New York, you have to wonder if these people forgot to take their meds, or if they're just expressing their artistic side.

But one thing is certain. The man who torments subway goers by squawking painfully on his saxophone while simultaneously declaring he hails from outer space has, at some point, taken a cab. Or, for that matter, driven one. When you step into a cab decorated with hundreds of Christmas lights and don't bat an eye, you will know you are a New Yorker.

RED LIGHT DISTRICT

~

Stoned, drunk, and drenched from a 2 a.m. downpour, Tina Tartillo*
and her friend Roy sought shelter from the storm in a Chelsea pizza
parlor, inhaling pepperoni-scented air while puddles formed around
their shoes. Looking out the window, she willed their friend Cody to
hurry up and return from his dealer's apartment with a fresh bag of
weed in hand.

"Where is he?" Tina said. Cold and wet, all she wanted was to go
back to the party, borrow a blow dryer and change into dry clothes. The
drenching had destroyed her good mood.

Cody finally reappeared, and Tina and Roy dashed into the rain
to meet him.

"What took you so long? It's been half an hour!" Tina asked. Cody's
eyes were glazed over like Krispy Kreme donuts. She sighed.

"Let's get a cab and get out of the rain."

Probably because they wanted a cab so desperately, Murphy's Law
went into effect and they saw zero empty taxis for ten wet, miserable
minutes. Finally, an available cab pulled over.

Roy jerked open the door and they piled into the back, Tina sitting
in the middle.

The cab driver, a slim man who didn't seem much older than Tina
turned towards them, his smile wide and his arms outstretched in a
sign of welcome. He stuck his face through the partition.

"Welcome to my cab!" he said exuberantly, as if welcoming them
to his mansion.

Tina hadn't noticed the lights until this moment. The front of the
cab practically glowed red. The cabbie had strung three or four strands
of Christmas lights across the dashboard, and a couple more framed
the windshield. Yet another two strands wove around the ceiling and
hung in front of the partition. Almost all the bulbs were red, although
the driver had switched out a few for orange or yellow. It was like
sitting in one of those Indian restaurants on East Sixth Street, where

literally every inch of the ceiling and walls were papered with brightly lit bulbs.

Some of the lights flashed, giving the illusion of moving in space, and Tina's stoned brain could barely handle it. She drew her attention away from the lights, instead zooming in on the rear-view mirror, only to become fascinated by what may have been a large color picture in an exotic frame—or perhaps a religions symbol—hanging from it.

The friends looked at each other, eyes wide, and then back at the cabbie.

"Welcome to my cab," their driver repeated.

His smile shone as brightly as the lights and his cheer was genuine. Much too genuine, Tina thought, for someone driving a cab at 2:30 a.m. on a rainy Friday night.

"This is a Happy Cab," the driver said. "You get in my cab and you're happy. I like my customers to be happy in my cab. Where are you going? Where are you going? I'll take you where you go. I'll take you anywhere you want to go."

Tina collected her thoughts. She was not happy, nor did she have any intention of becoming happy. Her clothes were heavy with rain, and her hair stuck to her head. She felt cold. Also, she was missing what had been a fun party.

"Uhh, we're going to Second and B."

The driver turned around and put his hands on the wheel.

"Okay, good, we go there."

He pulled out into the street, reached for his radio, and turned up the music. The song sounded like something out of a Bollywood movie, with Americanized electronic beats and samples underlying a traditional Indian melody. Tina discerned the beat of tabla drums and other traditional instruments. A saccharine-sweet female voice rose over the other instruments.

More comfortable with biting sarcasm and dead baby jokes than Happy Cabs, Tina turned to her friends and started talking. They talked about the weed Cody bought, about the party and who would probably still be there when they got back. But it was hard to concentrate. The lights, for one thing, were distracting. Especially for the guys. Unlike Tina, who grew up in Connecticut and frequently visited family in New York, the guys moved to the city from Texas a couple months ago. Tina doubted they were used to seeing people from India or the Middle East, period, let alone a red, glowing cab.

Tina, on the other hand, thrived on bizarre situations. Living in the city that never sleeps, the unexpected became the norm; she frequently felt like a character in a Fellini movie, like these situations couldn't be real life.

The driver looked at them through the rear view mirror and turned up the stereo.

"You like this song, you like this music, you like this?"

Tina embraced her role as the official spokeswoman.

"Yeah, it's great," she said, knowing she sounded sarcastic.

In her mind, Bollywood films were mostly to make fun of, but the cab driver took her sarcasm as encouragement.

"I tell you the story, I tell you the story."

"Ok, great."

Still sarcastic.

He told them the story of the song. It was about a young man and woman who fell in love, but who were separated because their families were feuding. The couple could only see each other at night, in secret. They would meet at a nearby river, where they could see each other's reflection in the water. The cabbie told them how the pair would look at each other in the moonlight and look at their reflections in the water. But still, they could not be together.

"It's such a story," he said. "Listen. You can hear the moonlight. She's singing about the moonlight."

"Okay," Tina replied, but with less venom than before.

The driver apparently felt his passengers hadn't grasped the song's beauty, because he proceeded to tell the story four more times. During the second retelling, Tina realized she listened more closely, in spite of herself. The third time, both Cody and Roy nodded at appropriate points in his story, vocalizing their agreement with the driver. By the fourth retelling, Tina found the driver's accent compelling, his cadence and the passion behind his words mesmerizing.

She had to admire someone who could keep up such unrelenting cheer. This wasn't just a scam to score big tips from tourists. She respected that, and in doing so, she started to open up, finding his goodwill infectious. In a city where angry parents use baby strollers to barrel down slow walkers, this man genuinely wanted them to be happy.

By the time the cabbie pulled up to their destination, the three sat in awe. They had stopped talking amongst themselves long ago.

They tipped him ten bucks on a fifteen-dollar fare.

As they got out, Tina said, "Thank you. This is by far the best cab ride we ever had. Thank you so much."

DANCE PARTY PEDICAB

~

Bill Bell wasn't surprised that the L subway line had stopped running. For the past two years, the city had regularly shut down the L train after midnight or for entire weekends, as city workers retrofitted the trains to run via computers instead of by conductors. Bill only cared about robot-operated trains in sci-fi films. Drunk and tired from his bartending shift, he fumed because at 12:30 a.m. on a Saturday morning, he was stranded in Manhattan without a subway home.

He wasn't alone in his predicament. He walked up the subway steps to the street, and saw three other people looking just as pissed off as he was.

"You guys going to Williamsburg?" Bill asked.

They were. They decided to share a cab.

The city was crowded and empty cabs were scarce, but eventually one pulled over. Bill and two others climbed into the back seat. The fourth member of their group sat up front with the driver, a young, clean-shaven South Asian man wearing a backwards baseball cap.

The cab's stereo blared what Bill, a musician, coined Pakistani party music. He'd heard it before at falafel stands and on Atlantic Avenue. Driven by synthesizers and a 1980s dance beat, the melody was carried by traditional instruments and velvety singing. The stereo was loud enough that Bill half expected sultry women in colorful saris to appear and whisk him off to a Bhangra dance party.

The music was so loud they couldn't talk, but they were too focused on the driver to care.

The cabbie was gyrating in his seat like Justin Timberlake. His body moved back and forth while his shoulders snaked from side to side. Bill hoped the seat-dance wouldn't prevent the cabbie from seeing the double-parked car straight ahead. They swerved around it.

The driver began bobbing his head back and forth to the music in an exaggerated fashion. He was headbanging without the long hair. The driver clearly felt the songs on a deep level.

Bill and the other passengers exchanged tentative looks out of the corners of their eyes. The driver began slamming on the brakes to the beat. Bill's head whipped back and forth.

This shit is not right, he thought, bracing himself.

The cab approached the Williamsburg Bridge, which stretched one-and-a-half-miles across the East River, and the driver continued his bobbing and weaving to the beat.

Bill's hands felt clammy at the thought of this guy driving them across the river. He noticed the other passengers looking awkwardly out the windows. He decided not to think about the driver, and to push

THE TAXICAB RIDER BILL OF RIGHTS

~

Much as the Bill of Rights gives American citizens freedom of speech, the Taxicab Rider Bill of Rights—often fastened to the back of the driver's seat—gives riders freedom *from* speech, or more specifically, the right to a radio-free trip. Under the Bill of Rights, passengers may demand drivers stump out lit cigarettes and ditch any burning incense. Unless there is danger, passengers have a right to a ride free from horn honking. Did your driver gun it through three red lights and jump a couple of curbs? This is also against the rules, as they're required to obey all traffic laws.

Something that will surprise many New Yorkers: they are guaranteed an "English-speaking driver who knows the streets in Manhattan and the way to major destinations in other boroughs." English-speaking? This is clearly a relative term, based on reports of some drivers grappling with terms like "left" and "right"—annoying, yes, but not a huge problem as finger pointing often seems the more accurate means of communication anyway. And as any Brooklyn resident can attest, giving your driver spotless and detailed directions is the only way you will ever get home. Otherwise, you and the cabbie will scale the streets until both of you grow old and withered.

aside the image in his mind's eye of their yellow car hurling over the side of the bridge. Better to think about playing guitar. Better to think about the cute girl he served that night. Hell, it would be better to think about alcohol poisoning than about this guy launching them into space.

About a quarter of the way across the bridge, the driver slammed his foot on the accelerator. It was late at night and traffic was light, so the car flew forward. Bill felt his body pulled back into the seat as they sped up. He had no idea how fast they were going. He didn't want to know. He felt ill.

He glanced quickly towards the cabbie, then did a double take, staring hard.

The cabbie was steering the car with his two bare feet. His hands were nowhere in sight.

Bill tried to swallow but couldn't. He kept staring.

The driver had placed his feet on either side of the steering wheel, which his toes failed to grip. Although his knees were up around his ears, he still managed to bob his head to the music. Bill wished that the cabbie's hands would magically appear on the wheel.

"Oh my God," Bill groaned. "Please let me make it home in one piece."

The other three passengers noticed the hands-less driver within seconds of each other. The woman sitting up front slowly turned her head towards the backseat, mouth slightly open, eyes wide. She made eye contact with Bill.

Bill then turned to the guy beside him, who looked just as shocked. After their silent acknowledgement that something went horribly wrong, they broke eye contact. The woman turned to again face forward in the front seat, and Bill looked out the right-hand window.

The driver chose this moment to begin gyrating his hips again. This action moved his legs, and by extension, his feet, causing the car to swerve erratically into the empty adjacent lanes. Bill's stomach churned and his psyche verged on mutiny. He kept quiet, figuring it would not be conducive to their personal safety to distract the driver from whatever planet he was on.

It only got worse when Bill realized the driver's feet weren't anywhere near the brakes. If they needed to stop quickly for some reason, it wouldn't happen. Yes, stopping would be impossible. They were as good as road kill. Bill could only focus on the guardrail that separated him from a steep drop and a cold swim in the churning river.

At last they reached the exit at the end of the bridge and the driver put his feet back down and his hands reappeared on the wheel. Bill exhaled and inhaled for the first time in what seemed like ages. He wondered if the guy regularly crossed bridges like this.

They drove the rest of the way without incident. The four strangers paid and tipped the guy. The cabbie drove away and no one spoke. They just parted ways.

JUSTICE

~

Doan Hoang bolted down the stairs, a flustered mess. She was running late for her job as a receptionist and office manager of a greeting card company. Once again, she had stayed up late fighting with her boyfriend, Nathan. She often blamed her lack of punctuality on their spats. That and the fact that Nathan's cat, named Nancy Whiskey after a local bar, had learned to unplug their alarm clock.

But in the back of her mind, she knew she was just habitually late, and would continue to be late even if the cat learned to make her buttered toast and lay out her clothes the night before.

Banging through the front door in the chilly November morning, Doan knew she needed to be seated at her desk within the next ten minutes —a problem, as she lived a twenty-five-minute walk away and the East Village offered no viable subway options. She had walked two blocks to Second Avenue and Fourth Street when she saw an open cab. Although her wallet always seemed too thin, she flagged it down.

"I'm going to 134 Spring Street in SoHo via Houston," she told the African driver.

The cab sped off. But instead of taking Houston, the main thoroughfare, he took Prince Street and got stuck behind a garbage truck.

Frustrated, she watched the meter tick as the cab sat idle behind the putrid garbage truck. She started doing the math in her head. She earned $23,000 a year. She could barely afford the rent on the 400-square foot one-bedroom she shared with Nathan and his best friend, who slept in the living room. The taxi's meter kept clicking. She knew she barely had enough money to spring for this cab ride in the first place, and now she was paying extra because the idiot driver couldn't follow her simple instructions. She snapped.

"I told you to take Houston, and you took Prince, and now we're stuck!" she yelled at the cabbie.

The driver didn't take her early-morning reprimand well. He scowled and shook his fist at her through the rear-view mirror.

Oh shit, Doan thought.

She didn't say another word for the rest of the trip. But despite her silence, the driver kept raising his fist and shaking it at her.

"Bitch don't know nothing," he muttered a number of times under his breath, his black eyes boring into her through the rearview mirror.

Afraid of the driver, Doan averted her eyes from him, wondering how she got into this situation.

The cabbie eventually passed the garbage truck and arrived at Doan's office. Doan paid up and out of habit left him a tip, a quarter.

The cab driver held the quarter in his hand. His fist tightened over it. He turned to Doan, scowling, drew back his fist and flung the quarter at her, through the partition. She instinctively flinched and closed her eyes. The quarter bounced off her chest.

Horrified, Doan jumped out of the car and ran towards her office. The cab driver sprang from his seat and chased her. Doan rushed up the sidewalk and, thankful for her head start on the driver, ran through the office's glass doors and locked them behind her.

The driver stood at the door shaking his fist at her. Like a bird teasing an indoor cat through the window, Doan turned around and gave the driver the finger. Tall and strong, he raised both fists above his head and shook them.

He yelled words she couldn't understand, although she read his threatening expression perfectly well. Doan took paper and pen out of her purse and while the driver yelled at her through the glass, looked past him to his taxi. She found the medallion number and wrote it down. She glared at the driver and flipped him off one last time and then ran upstairs.

Later that afternoon, Doan created a report of the incident and faxed it to the Taxi and Limousine Commission (TLC). She was awarded with a court date for the following January.

When the day came, Doan had no inkling of what to expect but she did know how to play her part. And this meant working hard to perfect her appearance. Her family was from Vietnam, but Doan grew up in Kentucky and had mastered the charming ways of Southern women. She tried to look as sweet and conservative as she could. She neatly fixed her short bob and showed off her slender figure with a dark blue A-line dress and a matching fitted blazer. She chose to wear blue after hearing that the color projected innocence.

Chances are, Doan's cabbie knew what to expect from his court appearance. Many drivers curse the TLC using the same language Americans reserve for rants against the Taliban. Drivers also believe they would have a better chance of coming out of Guántnamo Bay scot-free than exiting a TLC courtroom without a fine. So while Doan viewed the hearing as her path to justice, her driver probably heard the call "dead man walking" in the back of his mind.

During the subway ride to the trial, Doan clenched and unclenched her jaw. Nathan came with her, and she reached for his hand. The night Doan met Nathan, a performance artist, he was sitting onstage eating one dozen donuts and drinking a whole bottle of wine while reciting, "This is my body, this is my blood," until he vomited. She figured any man comfortable doing that should provide good moral support in a TLC courtroom.

Doan and Nathan reached the building and took the elevator to the warren of offices referred to as "the court." Doan's stomach tightened as her nervousness about the hearing and about seeing the driver again increased. They sat outside in a waiting room until someone called Doan's name.

They entered the courtroom, which was the size of an office. It was windowless with shiny mint green walls. It looked like a depressing amalgamation of a hospital, a funeral home and a courtroom.

The judge, a slim red-headed man in a suit, sat behind a large metal desk holding a tape recorder. There were a few metal chairs, two of which Doan and Nathan took. Then the cabbie walked in. While Doan had dressed up, the cabbie looked like a taxi driver, wearing a beige jacket, layers of plaid shirts, a T-shirt and khakis. He took another chair, but the room was so cramped that he had no choice but to sit one foot away from Doan.

The whole process took about twenty minutes.

She wasn't as afraid of the cabbie with Nathan beside her, but she wanted to win her case. Doan pegged the judge as a nice, white, sympathetic, middle-class intellectual and decided to milk it. She got into her role by recalling her fear when the cabbie shook his fist at her, when he glared at her, and when he chased her to her office.

Taxi Court

~

The Taxi and Limousine Commission (TLC) court is where angry passengers and enraged taxi drivers face off before an administrative law judge. Did the driver insult your lap dog? Refuse to take you to Washington Heights? Run a stop sign to scare you? Taxi court could be your next stop.

The vast majority of the TLC's cases are called in favor of the passengers. Needless to say, drivers hate taxi court. "I'd rather be in Guantánamo Bay," said driver John McDonagh. One of John's cabbie friends recently won a victory in the court, but it is one of the few John has heard of in his thirty years as a driver. But it's not just the slim chance of victory drivers hate. They also need to take time off work to be there.

Many drivers have issues, some cultural, that don't endear them to the court. They don't know to dress to impress a judge; some have body odor. Often, a language barrier can be a driver's downfall.

The TLC holds that passengers willing to go through the necessary ordeal to get a cabbie into court must have genuine grievances. True, it's no cake walk. Offended passengers need to fill out a slew of paperwork, wait months for a court date, get affidavits from witnesses and take time off work to testify. No small order.

It's one of the few courts where even lawyers can't call themselves winners, because few people think to hire them beforehand.

The judge hit record on the tape player, and as Doan told her story, she started to cry. The cramped room fed into the panic she remembered. She purposely made her voice shake and rise a few notches while dramatically recounting her experience, "... and then he threw the quarter at me, and I ran away, and I was so scared."

The judge listened patiently, making sympathetic noises. His calm gaze gave her confidence. Then the judge turned to the cab driver, who said he was from Ghana. Doan felt the cold of her metal chair beneath her short skirt. The cab driver stood up.

"She went like this," he said, holding up his middle finger, attempting to foil Doan's polished veneer of innocence.

Doan batted her eyelashes and sweetly replied, "That was after I jumped out of the car and ran away!"

The judge made an immediate judgment after the testimony. He fined the cabbie five hundred dollars for attacking Doan with the quarter. The driver looked furious. The judge told the driver that he had to come up with the money by the end of that day or the TLC would revoke his hack license until the commission received payment.

"Ha! Who's the tough guy now?" Doan thought, holding back a grin and her urge to do a victory dance.

As she and her boyfriend walked away, Nathan said, "I kind of feel sorry for him."

HIGH-HEELED BOYS

~

Late one hot summer night in the mid-1980s, Ryan Weidman was cruising the seedy Meatpacking District in Manhattan when four transvestite prostitutes hailed his cab.

Transvestite hookers were some of Ryan's favorite clients. He admired the way they lived on society's fringe and was drawn to their outcast status, the danger of their jobs and their illicit lifestyle. He also found them visually interesting, with their sexy, feminine clothes, the heavy make-up, broad shoulders and large hands. He befriended some of them. A professional photographer, he sometimes took their pictures when they rode in his cab. Whenever he did this, he'd give them a copy of the photo.

The trannies wore come-on attire. They snaked into low-cut shirts and short, tight skirts. Their bodies were large and manly and muscles rippled through their arms, making Ryan feel lean. They completed their look with high heels, wigs and faces caked with foundation, eye shadow and bright lipstick.

Ryan recognized one of them. He had previously taken her photograph and given her a copy. He liked having repeat customers in his cab. A familiar face also gave him a sense of security.

"Hey ladies," he said. "Be free, loosen up."

It was always a better trip for him when people had fun.

"Where you headed?"

They wanted to go to Harlem, but refused to give Ryan an exact address. Other cabbies would have kicked them out immediately. No specific destination indicated that the passenger was seeking a dark and abandoned corner to hold a knife to the driver's throat and rob him. But Ryan ignored this thought. He drove towards northern Manhattan, listening to music on the radio.

"Hey, change the radio station," one of the trannies said.

Her voice wasn't friendly.

Ryan noted the pushiness and didn't appreciate it. But he wanted a big tip so he changed the station. Also, he rationalized, there were four of them, and they were buff.

After driving more than one hundred blocks, they reached Harlem.

"We changed our mind," said one of the trannies. "We want to go to Brownsville."

Once again, they refused to give him an address.

The change of plans pissed off Weideman, and a kernel of worry began forming in his mind. Maybe something was going on that he didn't know about. The dollar figure on the meter was nearing fifteen dollars, but if he kicked them out now they may not pay up. Brownsville, deep in the heart of Brooklyn, may as well have lain on the other side of the world. Granted, it had much in common with Harlem, namely gang violence, drug pushers and scared families. But Ryan appreciated the dirty underside of life, and he enjoyed taking risks.

He shot down the freeway towards Brownsville. By now it was around 6 or 6:30 a.m., and the sun was rising. After thirty minutes of driving, they arrived in Brownsville. Ryan knew the neighborhood—he had a hooker friend who frequently needed a lift there—but the trannies took him through a vast labyrinth of streets until he no longer recognized his surroundings.

"Take a right here," they said. "Go to the corner. Take a left here."

It went on and on.

He came to a stop sign. On the other side of the street sat a cop car. That was okay with him. Ryan usually derided cops, but this time he felt good having them there. His relief at seeing the cop forced him to realize how uncomfortable this ride made him.

As he pushed his foot against the gas pedal, he looked in the rearview mirror. Until now, the trannies had been talking in the backseat. But with the police across the street they sat stone still, their eyes downcast. He immediately sensed that something was wrong. It was like feeling the presence of someone's eyes boring into the back of your head, or knowing who is on the other end of the line before picking up the phone. But he kept driving. The cop car disappeared as he turned a corner.

Ryan briefly thought about jumping out of his car and running after the cop and yelling, "I'm feeling something odd, something's not right!"

But he didn't. He didn't really trust his instincts. Plus, he wasn't the usual victim. People sensed his temper and sensed he got mean. Instead, he kept driving. His stomach rose towards his throat.

"Take a right here," one of the trannies commanded.

After a few more turns, one of them told him to stop in front of an old walk-up building. They quickly opened the doors and slid out.

"Hey, that's thirty-five dollars!" Ryan said.

None of them reached for money in their bras or skirts. Ryan realized they never planned on paying.

He got out of the car, unfolding himself to his full wiry height of over six feet.

"Hey, you owe me money!" he said threateningly.

The biggest trannie in the group walked up to Ryan. She towered over him with her high heels, and she was unquestionably thicker and more muscular than he was. She stared him down and without hesitating pulled off a stiletto.

Before he knew what happened, she whipped the shoe towards his head, stopping at the last second and holding the narrow heel threateningly to his temple. She brandished it like a weapon, like she knew what she was doing. She had done this before.

Ryan didn't fight her. He could see that her shoe would do serious damage to his head. It would be a disaster if she got him in the eye. The trannie continued to maintain eye contact. She seemed to dare him to move while her friends ran inside the house. Then, with one last sneer, she lowered the shoe and ran into the building.

Ryan jumped back in his taxi, gunned it, and traced his turns backwards looking for the cop. He hoped the police car was still there.

It was. He parked his cab and ran up to the cops.

"I've just been robbed!" he yelled.

He told the cops about the trannies, the stiletto and not getting paid.

"How much was on the meter?" one cop asked.

"Thirty-five dollars," he answered.

"Let's go," the cop said. "Lead the way."

The cop followed Ryan back to the building. Ryan stayed in the cab; the cop went to the door. He banged on the door. No answer. He banged on the door again. No answer. Again. No answer. Out of patience, the cop threw his body against the door and it crashed inwards. He ran inside the house. Ryan waited anxiously outside.

Five minutes later, the cop came out of the building. He walked up to Ryan's cab and gave him a handful of money. Ryan counted thirty-five dollars.

"Thanks," he said.

"You're welcome," the cop said. He turned around, and went back to his patrol car.

OFF BROADWAY

~

Iva Pekárková was in a hurry. She negotiated traffic and worried about getting her fare where she needed to go as soon as possible. When she turned from Sixth Avenue onto Central Park South, she was so distracted by her thoughts that she ran a red light. She heard the siren's blare behind her, saw the cop car's flashing lights and pulled over.

Iva's heart rate sped up. She was scared. She didn't have a lot of money, and tickets were expensive.

She turned to the woman in the back seat.

"Oh my God, I don't have the money to pay the ticket," she said in her Czech-accented English. "Please, try and help me. Please try to tell him you were in a hurry."

"Okay, no problem," answered the woman, who looked to be in her mid-thirties.

The cop came to the window. He asked for Iva's license and registration.

Iva didn't have a chance to respond to the officer before she heard an irate voice come from behind her.

"Finally I get a decent taxi driver who knows where she's going, one who's nice to me, and you pull her over!" screeched the woman in the backseat, showering the cop with her wrath. "And for what? I didn't see any red light!"

The woman continued to berate the policeman while simultaneously complimenting Iva.

It worked.

The policeman, confused and abashed by the onslaught of abuse, walked away without writing Iva a ticket.

Iva pulled away from the curb and laughed with relief.

"Thank you so much," she said to the woman. "That was so wonderful!"

"No problem," her passenger said. The two started chatting.

"So what do you do in life?" Iva asked.

"I'm an actress," the woman said.

CHAPTER 3

HERO WORSHIP

Superheroes Sans Tights and Capes

Gotham needs a hero. Batman would fit the bill, but unfortunately he's a comic strip character and, therefore, disqualified for being imaginary.

Someone *real* has to rescue this overcast city. Someone needs to foil the purse-snatcher and return the diamonds. Someone needs to get the puking drunk girl safely home. Someone needs to wear Batman's cape.

On occasion, cabbies step into this role.

They fit the classic hero formula. Not Joseph Campbell's formula—they don't have much of a chance to confront their fathers while driving a cab, after all. Rather, cabbies personify the hero whose gruff exterior masks a kind heart.

The reasons are multifold. First, when cabbies help their sick passengers, they take care of strangers. Someone who speeds his ill wife to the hospital has a vested interest in the situation. Cabbies don't know passengers and their acts to help others are those of selfless good Samaritans.

Second, it costs a cabbie money to help someone. If you absentmindedly leave your passport in their cab, and the driver hunts you down to return it, they lose money on gas (it's out of pocket) as well as on a fare. Generosity exemplified.

Third, like any good hero, the taxi driver is the underdog. Spiderman? A dorky science nerd. Wolverine? A sickly Canadian named James. Few can resist the story of the poor, immigrant cabbie, surviving on four-dollar meals, who sacrifices his time and energy to save a litter of puppies.

And last, yellow cab drivers—much like the Empire State Building and Saks—symbolize New York. When this gruff emblem of Gotham makes good and shows a softly beating heart, New Yorkers feel proud of humanity and our city.

Of course, cabbies occasionally play the villain. Taxi drivers with dilated pupils brandish hidden weapons or throw the first punch. In this instance, someone else has to rescue Gotham.

NIGHT ON THE TOWN

~

With a double shift behind the wheel and oppressive New York City heat dogging him, Stephen Joseph wrapped up his shift at 4 a.m. Only the thought of his apartment and his bed a couple blocks away kept him going. He could barely muster the energy to step on the brake as he came to a red light at the corner of Fourteenth Street and Park Avenue South, near Union Square.

He wasn't looking for fares when the three girls disregarded his off-duty light and ran screaming up to his cab. Two of the girls carried a boy between them, his arms wrapped around their shoulders and his feet dangled towards the ground.

Stephen grew up in New York and could tell the girls had been out for a night on the town. It was 1982, and the girls, who looked about eighteen, wore miniskirts and had fluffed and moussed their long, curly black hair. The boy appeared to be unconscious, although he seemed to be trying to move his feet to walk.

He rolled down the window. "Listen, I'm off duty," he said.

"No, no, he's been stabbed," one of the girls wailed hysterically. "He's been stabbed!"

Stephen looked at the boy, and for the first time saw the gaping, bloodless wound in his hairless chest. One of the girls held his bloody T-shirt, soaked so completely that Stephen couldn't make out the shirt's original color.

"Can you please take him to the hospital?" she begged, crying.

In the 1980s, New York City symbolized urban decay with a well-earned reputation for gang violence, crack, organized crime and murder. Times Square housed hookers and seedy strip joints instead of Toys 'R' Us and the ESPN sports bar. The Lower East Side—today known for nouveau American cuisine and overpriced vintage shops—was known for heavy drug activity and guns. In fact, according to FBI statistics, between 1982 and 2007, New York's murder rate plunged by seventy percent, and the number of robberies plummeted seventy-seven percent from 95,944 to 21,787 per year. A total of 107,430 vehicles were reported stolen in 1982, compared with 13,256 in 2007.

Although he had never been robbed or menaced, Stephen recognized the danger he faced as a cabbie. He was always a little afraid, and always wary. He was careful of who he picked up. If two or three guys wearing sneakers and hoodies standing near the Lower East Side's housing projects tried to hail him, he would drive right by.

"I wasn't worried about being politically correct," he said. "It wasn't based on color, it was based on class. It was where they were, how they were standing, how they were dressed, what time of night it was."

A native New Yorker who often worked in rough neighborhoods as an English teacher, Stephen knew what to avoid as a cabbie.

"In those days, there were a lot of hold-ups, there was violence against private cabs, and the gypsy cabbies were getting killed right and left," he said.

He had known one murdered cabbie. His friend's father was shot in the head during a robbery that took place at 116th Street and Second Avenue. The man died a couple of weeks later.

Despite his concerns, Stephen still occasionally picked up someone he considered "borderline," then spent the entire ride wondering when he'd get cracked over the head.

"It's a very strange feeling to have somebody sitting behind you," he said. "You have the feeling or sense that they could rob you or have a weapon. And you feel very helpless because you have your back turned."

His greatest fears as a driver were being killed or running over a pedestrian. He never considered the fact that someday, someone other than himself might die in his cab.

On the night of the stabbing, Stephen had already driven a double shift, and he expected to drive a total of thirty hours that weekend.

"I didn't say it, but my first thought was that he's going to bleed all over my cab and I'll have to clean it up," Stephen said. "It's not a very charitable thought, but it's what I thought."

But he knew he couldn't just drive away. He told them to get in. One girl clambered into the front seat, weeping. In the back seat, the other two crying girls held the silent boy in the back seat. He was Hispanic and looked about seventeen years old.

Stephen knew the area—he lived further down Fourteenth Street in Stuyvesant Town, a complex of often rent-controlled apartment buildings. The nearest hospital, Beth Israel, was about six blocks away.

"I floored it and went through all the lights, went left on Sixteenth Street, turned there and drove right up the ramp where the ambulances go," Stephen said. "Some workers came out and were waiting there. 'You can't come here, it's just for ambulances,' the workers yelled. I called out, 'I have somebody who's been very seriously injured, he got stabbed!'"

The hospital staff saw the boy, stopped arguing and grabbed a gurney. They hoisted the boy up, hurriedly tossed his bloody shirt on top of him, and rushed him into the building.

The girls begged Stephen to take them back to the club. The boy's brother had been stabbed, too, they said, and they needed to bring him to the hospital as well.

"I was already so upset at his point and I figured, whatever, what the hell," he said. "It was a five-minute ride. I couldn't say no."

When he neared the club, the cops had already arrived, red and blue lights flashing along the street. Stephen pulled up and a cop walked over.

"You can't get in here," the cop said.

Stephen explained that he came to pick up someone who was hurt, someone who needed to go to the hospital. The girls cried in his cab. The cop asked Stephen his name. He gave his real first name and lied about his last, saying it was Jacobs. He didn't want to get mixed up in legal issues—human issues were enough.

"I was hoping he wouldn't take my medallion or license number," Stephen said. "He didn't seem to—he just wrote whatever I told him in the book."

The cop informed them that an ambulance had already taken the boy's brother to the hospital. So Stephen backed up, turned around, and drove back to the hospital. On the way, the girls told him their story. They lived in the Bronx, and had brought the boy to the city as a treat. He had never been to a nightclub before, and they wanted to show him the ropes on a Saturday night. They told him to wear khakis and a T-shirt.

"The fight started over something really senseless," Stephen said. "It was some kind of argument over somebody making fun of one of the girls or his clothes."

The boy got in a pushing match with some other guys at the club, they went to square off, and the other guy—right in the middle of the club—pulled out a knife and plunged it into the boy's heart.

Stephen pulled up to the emergency room, and the girls rushed out. A nurse told them that the boy's brother had only been stabbed in the shoulder; the wound wasn't life-threatening. With the girls out of the cab and the boys in the hospital, Stephen could finally head home. He was almost there, anyway. He only lived one block from the hospital. In fact, he parked his car on the same block. He had planned on driving the next day—Sunday—but was too upset. Instead, he went to his friends' beach house near Atlantic Beach, ten miles east of Kennedy Airport. He wanted to find out what happened to the kid, so that afternoon he picked up the *New York Daily News*, late edition, and found the story. Apparently, a number of people were hurt in the brawl, but there was only one fatality, a fifteen-year-old who died of a stab wound. The kid.

The newspaper included the boy's address, and Stephen tracked down the family's phone number though information.

"I called their house a number of times the following night," he said. "I just wanted to tell whoever answered, his parents or whoever, that I had been involved and to give them my condolences, even though they were strangers."

But nobody answered. He never called again. Authorities never caught the guy who stabbed the boy.

Stephen doubts the boy was dead when he got in the cab. If he were, the two girls wouldn't have been able to hold him up, he theorizes. The boy would have been dead weight.

"I think he died in the cab," he said. After all, there was no blood in the taxi when they got out. "He'd already done all his bleeding."

Benefits of Ownership

~

The difference between drivers owning their own medallion and those driving for a garage that owns the medallion is comparable to the difference between buying and renting a home. It's another way of life.

Drivers who coughed up the cash for their medallions and their cabs have more control. If the city is dead or if the driver feels sick, they can ditch work and go home. If business is booming, they can stay out longer. But with more control comes more responsibility. Medallion owners are required by law to buy a brand-new car every five years or so, and they must pay for their own insurance and auto upkeep, and still pay off that medallion.

Those who drive for garages are, in many ways, slaves to the system. Many pay the garages more than one hundred dollars at the start of each shift to lease their cab. Some lease by the week, paying a bit less than those who lease by the day. But if rainy or cold weather keeps potential fares indoors, these drivers still must cruise for passengers—paying for their own gas—hoping to make enough money to make the shift worthwhile. Garages are not required to provide drivers with health insurance, disability insurance, retirement plans, or other benefits.

The TLC sanctioned leasing, or horse-hiring, in 1979.

THE DOCTOR

~

Taxi driver Abdul Rauf Chaudhry's fellow cabbies have a nickname for him—Dr. Rauf.

The Doctor, a middle-aged Pakistani man with kind eyes, earned his nickname six years ago on a warm spring afternoon. Just beginning his shift, Rauf drove his taxi from the Long Island City garage and had just reached Manhattan when he saw a slim man standing in the middle of the road, waving his arms at oncoming traffic. A silver Dodge van was parked on the right side of the road.

Thinking the man needed gas, Rauf pulled over his cab to help.

The man, who looked to be about twenty-five, ran up to Rauf's unrolled window. He was sweaty and nervous. Rauf pegged him as an Orthodox Jew because of his beard, yarmulke and side curls.

"My wife is having labor pains," he said, his voice soft but panicky. "Can you bring her to the hospital?" he pleaded, almost in tears.

He quickly agreed. "Yes, I'll take her."

"Can you help me bring her to your cab?" the man asked.

Rauf agreed and stepped out of his taxi. The father of six children, he easily recalled his fear the first time his wife gave birth. Rauf started towards the van and had only taken a few steps when he heard a scream that turned into a desperate wail. Rauf knew his wife sounded like that shortly before their children were born. He reasoned this woman's labor was advanced.

They reached the van's open sliding door and Rauf saw the man's wife sitting in one of two bucket seats in the back. Her face glistened with sweat and the hair beneath her head scarf was wet. A long skirt engulfed her small frame, and she looked very thin outside of her basketball-shaped belly. Tears ran down her cheeks. She briefly looked at Rauf but she didn't really seem to register his presence.

"I just want to lie down," she whimpered.

Despite the woman's slight build, Rauf doubted she could comfortably lie down in the back of his taxi. He imagined her with her arms cramped at her sides and her feet pressed against the door.

He turned to her husband. "The space is not good in my car," he said. "If you want she can lie in the back of the van or even on the side of the road. But if you think it best, I will bring her to my backseat."

Her husband didn't hesitate. "Let's take her to the cab."

The woman could barely walk, so the men stood on either side of her, each wrapping one arm around her back and hooking their other arm behind her knees. They carried her to the cab and placed her in the back seat.

Rauf, who didn't have a cell phone, looked at the guy and said, "Brother, call 911."

The man raised his hands helplessly, his face pale and scared. "I don't have a cell phone."

A contraction hit. The woman screamed and held her stomach. Her husband rushed to her, fear etched in his face.

"Please, please do something," he begged Rauf. "Take her to the hospital."

Rauf wasn't sure he should take her to the hospital. The city traffic would force him to brake quickly and change lanes sharply. If she gave birth while he wove through cars, he could jostle and hurt her or the baby as they lay helpless in the backseat.

Rauf had seen his wife give birth to his youngest sons, now eight and eleven, and he knew how to tell how far along she was. He walked up to the woman and looked under her skirt. She wasn't wearing anything underneath, and he could see she was very dilated. He made his decision.

"Driving with her is too dangerous," he told her husband.

"Please help us," the husband begged.

Rauf saw how young he looked. The guy was helpless in his panic.

Rauf collected his thoughts. He had gone to technical college in Pakistan before leaving to study in the Netherlands. While in the Netherlands he worked in a hospital, but he was no doctor. True, his wife had given birth many times, but he had never delivered a baby—that was the doctors' work.

The woman writhed in the backseat. Her screams barely let up. She was drenched in sweat and the veins popped in her forehead. Rauf could tell that the baby was about to come. He took a deep breath and tried to remember what the doctors in the hospital had done for his wife. He recalled that they told his wife to push and to breath. They also talked to her in comforting voices.

Rauf took a deep breath.

"We should take off her skirt," he instructed her husband.

He looked kindly at the woman.

"Breath," he said.

She looked at him like he was her lifeline, and she breathed when he told her.

"That's good, you will be good," he said softly.

The force of the next contraction hit and she howled in pain.

"Push!" Rauf coached. "Push, be strong, push!"

She squeezed her eyes shut with the effort.

"You don't have to worry," he reassured her. "It will be good."

For the next few minutes, Rauf alternately told her to breath and push. He tried to sooth her with comforting words.

Then he and the husband saw the baby's head crown.

"The baby's coming, the baby's coming, the baby's coming," Rauf said, as much to himself as to anyone else.

The woman's screams were constant. Rauf slid his fingers in and underneath the baby's head, supporting it, and told her to push. She looked exhausted, but she grimaced and bore down. Rauf slowly guided the head out. He told her to push again. She screamed and pushed. The baby's shoulders appeared. Rauf gently brought the child out. It was a boy.

His cab was a mess, but he didn't care. The brand-new baby lay in his hands. He cut the umbilical cord. Then he held the child with its stomach towards the ground, tilting its little head towards the floor in order to release anything that had gotten into baby's mouth or nose during the birth. He needed to make sure the child could breath. After holding him in that position for about forty-five seconds, the baby started to cry. He turned the baby boy over, and gently placed him on the mother's belly, by her breast. She smiled and wrapped one arm around her baby, gently stroking him. She looked exhausted, happy and relieved. So did her husband.

A voice came from behind Rauf, startling him.

"Doctor, come here, you don't have gloves and you have to wash your hands. That stuff can be toxic."

It was a cop. Rauf had no idea how long the officer was standing behind him. He heard an ambulance siren in the distance.

The presence of the cop jolted him. He hoped he hadn't done anything wrong or broken any laws by delivering the baby. He couldn't have handled the situation differently. He wondered if the cop would understand. And he wondered what the cop would say when he learned Rauf wasn't a doctor.

He followed the officer to his car. The cop pulled out cleansers to wash up with.

Rauf grew more nervous as the cop watched him wash his hands and arms. He knew that people without U.S. citizenship could be deported, and he hoped delivering the baby wouldn't give them a reason to send him away. He had Dutch citizenship, so he wouldn't have to go back to Pakistan, but he earned good money in the United States for his family. Yet he also knew that many of New York's Pakistani community had been singled out since 9/11, and he didn't want to be next. He wanted to stay.

As he finished washing up, Rauf told the cop the truth.

"I'm the cab driver," he said. "I'm not a doctor."

The cop looked confused. "How come you delivered the baby?"

"Because she was very, very dilated," he said. "And because two times in the hospital I saw my wife having babies."

The cop sized him up.

An ambulance had battled its way through the traffic and pulled up near the taxi. The paramedics jumped out and saw the woman lying in the back of the cab, playing with her newborn baby. Then one of the paramedics noticed Rauf.

"Who are you?" he asked. "Why are you standing here?"

"Listen," Rauf said, his fear ebbing and a bit of pride coming through.

"I did the whole job. It was me."

He motioned to his cab. The EMT looked momentarily confused, then his eyes widened as he caught on.

"Aha," he said.

The EMTs spoke briefly with the policeman. Then the cop asked Rauf for his name, address and phone number.

"Maybe we'll call you," he said.

They never did.

After wrapping up his short interview with the cop, Rauf walked over to the couple. They both looked down awkwardly and gave him small smiles. They seemed shy and humble. Rauf felt that they didn't know how to respond to all the strangers surrounding them at this intimate moment. He shook hands with the husband, and gave his best wishes to the wife and their child.

"I was very happy—I felt proud," Rauf said. "I was very glad that I could do that, that God helped me and that everything was good."

OUTER BOROUGH EXPERIENCE

~

The area of Cobble Hill near the Carroll subway stop was nearly deserted when Jason Barney came upstairs from the subway station. When he turned to walk towards his apartment, he saw a tall, blonde, bohemian guy standing under a streetlight and looking at a subway map. He wore a backpack and his expression was puzzled. No wonder. The subway map was upside down.

Jason walked up to the guy.

"Where are you trying to go?" he asked.

"Fort Green," he said in a northern European accent.

Jason knew the G train, which went directly from Cobble Hill to Fort Green, wasn't running because of construction. Not that the G ever ran consistently. The guy could walk the thirty minutes to Fort Green, but Jason was afraid he would make a wrong turn and find himself lost in Brooklyn's dodgier areas.

"You should really take a cab," Jason said. "Let me hail you one."

The two walked down Smith Street looking for a cab. Jason learned the tourist came from Germany, and that he was en route to a party held by art students studying at Fort Greene's Pratt Institute. After a few blocks, they saw a taxi and Jason held out his arm.

The taxi pulled over. Jason walked up to the driver's open window. "Would you take this man to Fort Greene?"

The cab driver didn't hesitate. "No," he said. The response didn't surprise Jason. Most drivers refused to go further into Brooklyn. Unless Brooklynites wanted a lift to Manhattan, it was often no dice.

But Jason, who had traveled widely through Asia and Latin America, and who had hitchhiked across the United States a few times, knew that money talked in almost all situations.

He walked to the cab and put his fingers on the open windowsill. He leaned in. "I will pay you to take this man to Fort Green," and said, reaching around to his back pocket for his wallet.

As Jason reached back, the cabbie quickly reacted. He leaned over towards the passenger side, fished around under the seat and pulled out a thick metal chain. Each link was the size of a steel fist and the whole chain was longer than a sword. If that heavy weapon made contact, the best case scenario was it would leave raised welts and raging bruises. In a worst case scenario, it would break someone's skull.

The cab driver held up his weapon and Jason stepped back. He put his arm in front of the tourist, the way mothers do to protect their children. They both stepped back to the sidewalk.

While the scene unfolded, the lyrics and beat of Thela Hun Ginjeet, a spoken-word story by prog rock fathers King Crimson, raced through Jason's head: "It's about New York City, it's about crime in the streets … So I walk around a corner/and I'm shaking like a leaf/ And I thought 'this is a dangerous place.'"

"Let's get out of here," Jason said, the song looping through his mind. The German guy, who hadn't yet seen the chain and who didn't have the best grasp of English, looked at Jason questioningly. He didn't move.

The cabbie opened his car door and got out. He stood at least six feet tall. He planted his feet shoulder-width apart and pulled his shoulders back. His dark eyes narrowed in anger. His jaw was set. He began swinging the chain from his hip.

Finally grasping the situation, the tourist's mouth dropped open, his eyebrows shot up, and he stepped back.

The driver stepped forward, swinging the chain. "Get away from my cab," he said menacingly.

But Jason didn't step away. A laid-back surfer and drummer from the Jersey Shore, he normally avoided confrontation. He didn't fight. But the cabbie needed to be put in his place. He decided to meet force with force. He stepped towards the driver.

"What's wrong with you?" he yelled, his anger rushing out. "This man only wanted a ride to Fort Greene! What are you doing?"

The driver continued to swing the chain, glaring menacingly.

"What are you going to do? Hit me?" Jason shouted. He was terrified of being mangled by the chain hurling through the air but consciously refused to show it. He hoped that his decision to fight back wouldn't get him and the tourist killed. "If you hit me, I might go to the hospital, but you will go to jail!"

The man continued silently swinging his chain and glaring at them, but he had stopped stepping towards them. Jason backed away and motioned the tourist to follow him. They turned around once Jason felt they were a safe distance from the cabbie. He looked back over his shoulder. The driver held his aggressive stance, the chain at his hip.

Jason and the tourist walked along Smith Street. They heard a car door slam. Then the offending cab driver drove past them, slowly, leering at them. Like in an Old West showdown, Jason met and held his gaze.

Seconds after the driver pulled out of sight, another cab drove up. Once again, Jason put his arm out. And once again, Jason approached the driver's open window.

"Can you take this man to Fort Greene?" he asked, feeling apprehensive and desperate to get the tourist where he needed to go.

"Sure, I'd be happy to," said the cab driver, who Jason could tell was a Sikh by his turban. This driver emanated a sense of warmth and kindness. "Get in."

The tourist got in and the cab sped off.

A few days later, Jason spoke with his ex-girlfriend, a Pratt student, on the phone. He gave her a play-by-play of the experience.

"Hey, I already heard this story!" she exclaimed.

"What?" asked Jason incredulously.

"Seriously! There was a German guy sitting in on one of my photography classes. He told the entire class his story. We couldn't believe it. And he had only been in New York for two weeks!"

THE DIAMOND MISER

~

When Osman Chowdhury opened his trunk to load his passengers' luggage, he saw the black bag sitting there. It must have been there for hours.

A picture of the woman who probably left it flashed through his mind. He had picked her and her friend up at Penn Station. Osman, forty-one years old with a slight potbelly, popped his trunk but stayed in his taxi while Penn Station's dispatcher loaded their luggage. The women, in their early thirties, were professionally dressed. One talked on her cell phone for most of the trip to the Hilton at Fifty-third Street and Sixth Avenue.

When Osman pulled up to the hotel, he popped the trunk for the doorman, who unloaded the luggage.

"That's ten dollars and seventy cents," he said to the women.

One of the women handed him a twenty. "I'll have nine dollars back," she said, leaving him thirty cents, or a 2.8 percent tip. Today, Osman claims the measly tip didn't bother him. But if all his customers tipped so stingily, he would pocket $1.80 an hour, or a total of $21.60 for a grueling twelve-hour day. The tip wouldn't even cover the cost of gas he used to take her to the hotel. Despite her miserly behavior, Osman felt bad for the women whose bag sat in his trunk. He knew he got upset if he lost ten dollars. He imagined how terrible it would be for her if something important or valuable were in the bag.

The three men who had just hailed his cab stood beside Osman, their suitcases nearby. They, too, spotted the abandoned bag in the trunk.

"Maybe it's a bomb," one of the men joked.

Osman, a Muslim born in Bangladesh, didn't laugh. He understood the man meant to be funny and that none of them actually thought it was a bomb. He had driven a cab for ten years, and since 9/11, an increasing number of passengers made comments that Osman took personally because of his heritage. If cops had overhead the words "bomb" and "bag" spoken near his cab, Osman felt he'd be in deep trouble.

As he loaded the guys' luggage into his cab, Osman cooked up a plan. He would first drop the men off at the airport and then try and locate the bag's owner. Importantly, he would call his union, the New York Taxi Workers Alliance, because of the bomb comment. He didn't want any problems.

As he drove to the airport, he thought about how he'd track down the bag's owner. He didn't want to go to the hotel. It was after 6 p.m., and chances were, a new doorman would be on duty. Even if the old doorman were there, he might not remember Osman or his passenger. And what if the woman had switched hotels? If he gave the bag to the doorman, she still may not get it back.

He sighed. It was so much easier returning lost cell phones. Their owners eventually called, and when Osman answered the phone they would pick a time and place to meet.

He knew he wouldn't go to the police precinct. He had done that before when a family left behind a bag. Not only did he get bounced from station to station, but in the end, the police refused to take the bag. In all, he wasted more than two hours of driving time.

After Osman dropped the guys off, he called the union offices on his cell phone. He knew the number well—he worked as an organizing committee member. Director Bhairavi Desai answered the line. Osman told her the story.

"Bring it in," Ms. Desai said.

He carried the bag into the union's small offices, where he met Ms. Desai. "Let's look for a phone number," Osman said. They found a tag with a phone number on it. Ms. Desai called the number—it was in Dallas, Texas—but no one answered.

"We should open up the bag," Ms. Desai suggested. "Maybe we can find information about the owner there."

They slid open the zipper. They found a stack of papers, a laptop, and two packages wrapped in dark blue silk. They saw no business cards or names.

Osman reached in to open one of the navy bags, and saw something glittering in a small case.

He pulled out the case and saw a number of diamond rings on display, their polished stones and gold bangs gleaming in the light. His hands shook and his breath caught in his throat.

"Oh my God," said Ms. Desai, looking at the bag. She rapidly called the Dallas number again.

LOST AND FOUND

~

Taxicab lost and found? Lost forever, more likely. According to a study by Manhattan Councilwoman Gale Brewer, "a New Yorker misfortunate enough to lose her property in a taxi is more likely to find overwhelmed hotlines and contradictory instructions than she is to recover her missing possession."

According to the TLC, the official way to hunt down your missing belongings is by calling the TLC hotline. However, in order for TLC reps to track your cabbie, they need the medallion number. So unless you kept a receipt or have the neurotic habit of scribbling down medallion numbers, the TLC leaves you SOL.

Another way to track missing goods is by calling the police precincts designated as official drop-offs for items lost in cabs. This method would be handier if more cab drivers bothered with police stations. As is, going to police precincts costs drivers money——they have to take time off the meter to drive there and file a police report. It's hardly surprising that many choose to cart lost items back to their garages, which generally have their own lost and founds.

Really, everything depends upon the upstanding nature of your cabbie, as well as that of the passengers picked up after you. Some drivers go out of their way to return items. One has a sure-fire way to track down anyone who lost a cell phone in his cab. He simply calls "Mom." You can always count on Mom knowing where her kids are.

Trembling, Osman reached for the second silk bag and slowly opened it. Inside, there was another, similar display case. As he pulled it out, more rows of sparkling diamond rings emerged. With his other hand, he reached for first case. He started counting. One, two, three . . . he had never held anything worth so much money in his life. Fourteen, fifteen, sixteen . . . oh, the poor woman, to have lost this many diamonds! Twenty-five, twenty-six, twenty-seven . . . it was as if someone had left a jewelry shop in his cab. He couldn't believe it.

There were thirty-one rings total. He counted them again.

"Oh God, she's going to have a heart attack when she realizes this is gone!" Osman said. "We have to find her!"

The bomb comment vanished from Osman's mind when he looked at the shimmering loot. But he had to protect himself. He had to make sure nobody accused him of stealing this bag and the diamonds. "I'm going to contact the media," Ms. Desai said.

Ms. Desai was calling the Dallas number again when a television crew from local TV station NY1 arrived. They agreed to do an exposé and help locate the diamonds' owners.

This time, someone in Dallas answered. "Who are you?" the woman on the other end of the line asked.

"I'm Bhairavi Desai with the New York Taxi Worker's Alliance, and my driver found a suitcase in his trunk. This number is on the tag."

"It's my daughter's!" the woman said.

"Can you help us find her?"

The mother apparently did just that. NY1's crew was still taping the exposé when a young woman walked through the Alliance's door. Osman recognized her as the one he dropped off at the Hilton. She was the woman who tipped him thirty cents.

"Who's the driver?" were the first words out of her mouth.

Osman stepped forward. "I am."

A wide smile spread across her face. "I have no way to describe how I'm feeling," she said. "I never thought I'd see that suitcase again."

Osman beamed.

"You probably think that I'm so stupid," she said.

"Oh, no no," Osman insisted.

The woman walked up to him. "So, are you married or single?" she asked.

"Single," he replied, not really understanding why she asked.

"Do you want jewelry or money?" she asked.

Osman hadn't really thought about a reward. He returned things all the time for people. Sometimes passengers didn't even pay his fare for delivering the item. But it was important to him to remain honest. He didn't come from much—both his parents died when he was young and he was raised by his sister in Bangladesh—but he didn't want to acquire wealth in a dishonorable way.

"I don't need anything," he said. "This makes me happy."

She wasn't so easily thwarted. "How much money do you make?"

"What do you mean?" Osman asked.

"How much do you make an hour?"

"Twenty-five dollars an hour," Osman said. Of course, if people tipped him thirty cents after a ten-minute ride he would make much less, but fortunately most New Yorkers were more generous.

The woman took her checkbook out of her handbag. She wrote out a check and handed it to Osman. It was for one hundred dollars and would cover slightly more than the driving time he lost. The woman said the rings were worth $30,000, in which case her one hundred dollars reward came to 0.33% of the bags' value. However, she may have underestimated the price—while Wal-Mart sells engagement rings for much less than $1,000, most rings with solitaires cost upwards of $5,000, which could bring the loot's total to $155,000.

Then she asked for his address and phone number, pledging to write to the Taxi and Limousine Commission and tell them about him. At this point, the NY1 journalists asked the woman for an interview. She wisely declined: No good could come from the labels "bad tipper" and "irresponsible diamond-loser."

NY1 ran the story of the returned diamonds without her interview, and the next day, a media frenzy bombarded Osman. Journalists from all over the country called. But when the BBC showed up, he was truly excited. This meant that his family in Bangladesh would see him. He hadn't seen his family since he moved to the United States at age nineteen in 1992, although he spoke to his sisters and brothers on the phone.

When the sister who raised him saw his image on the news, she called him in tears. She was so proud. He had brought a positive light to Bangladesh—a country more famous for politicians dipping their hands into relief money than for honesty. Articles in the Bangladeshi media asked their leaders to regard Osman as a role model.

Still, Osman insists that it was the most natural thing in the world to return the diamonds. And he's still not worried about the thirty-cent tip.

SPEED FREAK

~

Dan Ryder* is a bad boy turned good. As a taxi driver, he no longer runs scams at the airport, picking up confused passengers and charging them unholy amounts to drive them to distant terminals. He stopped hanging out with his buddy who invented a device to speed up the taximeter.

Nothing happened to precipitate this change. Dan, a man with a football player's breadth and a preference for leather trench coats, just woke up one morning, decided to go straight and didn't look back.

A couple years into his reformed ways, Dan Ryder got a call from radio dispatch at 6:15 a.m. on a Saturday.

"Hey, we need you pick someone up," his dispatcher said, adding that the women worked for a top news publication. "She lives in Planes, New Jersey. She needs a lift to JFK, then back to the publication's headquarters. We need you there by seven."

"No problem," Dan answered.

He took down the address, and drove the yellow cab towards New Jersey. He got off the exit to Scotch Plains, found the address and turned into the driveway. A woman came out the front door and got into his car.

"Hello," she said.

"Hello," he replied in a deep voice fitting his height—well over six feet—and the muscular breadth of his shoulders.

He backed out of the driveway and drove in the direction of the expressway. Once they reached the highway, his passenger leaned towards the front seat.

"I just wanted to explain that you driving me today is a very special job for my magazine," she said. She then introduced herself as the publication's photo editor. "We're waiting for photos from the Middle East, of the fighting between Iran and Iraq. The photos have been smuggled out of the Middle East, and you and I will be waiting for the Concord to fly them in."

These were physical photos on papers, not digital photos. Before the digital age, photojournalists planted themselves in the thick of wars or jungles and snapped images on film, constantly reloading their cameras. They then sent the negatives or the photos to their U.S.-based publications, often by plane. Important pictures that heralded breaking news were often zoomed in by Concord.

The editor explained the importance of these photos. It was the October 1980, and the photographers had risked their necks to take images from the rapidly escalating clashes between Iran and Iraq. Under cover, the photographers had infiltrated the border area and captured the violence and death on film.

"The pictures are for our cover story on the war," the photo editor continued. "We're holding the printers and keeping staff on call until I deliver them. So can you do me a favor? Once I have these photos, I'd like you to drive as fast as possible to our Manhattan offices. Time is essential."

"You have the right guy," Dan replied.

Yes, Dan had gone straight. But he refused to stop speeding. He lived for that rush.

A Brooklyn native in his twenties, Dan was known among his peers, dispatchers and bosses as a speed freak with cat-quick reflexes. He flashed across lanes and outmaneuvered New York's expressway traffic in a way that made some of the steeliest stomachs queasy. But people running late for important appointments praised him for their prompt arrival and for the fact that they arrived in one piece. These same customers often tipped him handsomely. He made good money. Dan's speedometer regularly hit one hundred mph.

Radar guns existed to catch speeders during the 1970s and early 1980s, but hadn't yet been appropriated by New York's cops, Dan believed. At the time, Dan went on the theory that cops clocked someone's speed by physically trailing behind the car—keeping pace speed-wise—for a quarter mile, then issuing a ticket accordingly. Dan developed his own method for beating this system. When he gunned it to one hundred mph, he would constantly check his mirrors for another car behind him, also speeding at one hundred mph and weaving through traffic. If he spotted such a car, he assumed it was a cop and slowed down before the quarter-mile point. "It was virtually impossible to get nailed if you were observant," he insisted.

The need for speed started early. In fact, Dan got his first speeding ticket in 1973, when he was caught going forty in a thirty-mph zone on Flatbush Avenue near Brooklyn's Prospect Park only two weeks after he got his probationary license. He suffered the consequences, paid a fine and had his temporary license suspended for a few months.

As a taxi driver, Dan equated speed with efficiency. And cash.

"The faster I finished my job and got back for the next one, the faster I made more money," he said.

He could have cared less about the speedometer, at least once he gunned it.

"Once I start to go one hundred or faster, I don't look at it," he said. "The speedometer won't hit you. Cars hit you. Speed isn't a numbers thing. I'm driving according to the roadway or the vehicles, or lack of vehicles, around me. The only reason I ever look at a speedometer is to avoid a speeding ticket. Staring at the speedometer will get you killed at any speed."

He's never had an accident while speeding.

"In fact, the only accidents I've ever been involved in were at low speeds, or when I've been hit," he said. "And I've driven over three million miles."

Once, in the late 1970s, Dan picked up a state trooper at Kennedy airport. The guy flashed his badge at Dan and asked him to step on it. Dan took off like a bullet, opening and closing gaps in the highway at speeds higher than one hundred mph. After about five minutes, the trooper asked him to join the force. Dan turned him down, but it didn't stop the trooper from trying to recruit Dan for the rest of the ride. But Dan remained adamant, knowing that joining the state police would have meant a salary cut.

Also, Dan would never have passed a drug test.

He never drank coffee or other caffeinated beverages to hype himself up for an aggressive drive. Rather, he smoked marijuana to help him deal with the pressure of it all.

"I actually focused more intensely on driving" after smoking weed, he said. "I enjoyed it more. It enabled me to do high-speed maneuvers easily in close quarters, with only a few inches here and there for clearance."

In fact, he had smoked a couple joints before picking up the state trooper.

"He never knew the difference," Dan said.

Dan drove in silence with the photo editor through New Jersey to Queens. Once they reached Kennedy Airport, Dan put the car in park in front of the "Arrivals" area. Then they began to wait, in silence, for the plane to touch down.

They sat for three hours. The editor stayed still but looked tense. She knew she needed those photos. She also knew that if the photos didn't get in pronto, it meant trouble. The publication had to be closed on time. They had to put it to bed. If they missed that deadline, they missed their distributors. If they missed their distributors, they missed time on the newsstand. If they missed time on the newsstand they pissed off their advertisers. Pissed off advertisers spent less money, and it would be on her head.

Finally, the Concord landed. Dan doesn't remember how the courier and the editor found each other in the days before cell phones—maybe she went inside the airport to meet him, or maybe he came outside looking for the rented limo—but they met up. The courier got into his taxi, giving the photo editor the proof she needed that the Iran-Iraq War was on.

"How fast can you get to Midtown?" the editor asked Dan. "We're going to Madison and Forty-fifth."

"You have the right driver," he answered. "But you may not be able to take it. You may want to close your eyes."

He gunned the taxi out of the airport, accelerated onto the freeway and held steady around one hundred mph while weaving through traffic. The editor watched the whole time and didn't say a word.

"She took it like a trooper," he said.

It only took Dan thirteen minutes to drive to Manhattan. It took him another five minutes to reach the magazine's Midtown offices, including stop signs and red lights.

When he pulled to a stop in front of her building, the editor handed him the fee as well as money for the tip. But Dan's employer had a no tipping policy; Dan still sped because he took pride in his job, not just for the cash. He was determined to stay straight. He was like an alcoholic—it was all or nothing and he badly wanted to stay clean. He handed her the tip back.

"I'm sorry, but we're not allowed to accept tips," he said.

"No, really, take it," she urged.

"I can't do that," he said. "It's company policy."

She relented, took back the money and got out of the car.

Dan drove down the street, but hadn't gotten further than a couple of miles before his boss radioed him.

"Hey, the editor called me," he said. "She pretty much demanded that you accept this tip. Go back there and pick up your tip. She insisted."

Dan did just that. When he reached the building, the editor came outside, both her hands full of wadded up cash. A mound of money.

"I took up a collection around the office," she said.

Her staff, impressed with Dan's driving dexterity, relieved to put the publication to bed, and excited to spend the rest of their Saturday outside the office, had happily tossed money into the pile.

The editor handed Dan the crumpled bills, thanked him, and walked back into the building.

CHAPTER 4

REMARKABLE ENCOUNTERS

Fares with Wisdom and Sometimes Fame

Life-altering moments happen in taxicabs. Sometimes these moments are obvious—like a marriage proposal in the backseat. Other times, the moment is only recognized as pivotal after the fact, like when a developing Bonnie and Clyde rips off their first cabbie.

As odds go, it's likely more drivers than passengers experience these reality jolts in taxis, if only because drivers spend sixty hours a week holed up in their metal second homes. But it's the passengers I spoke with who readily recalled the unexpectedly poignant moments they shared with their drivers. Generally, passengers' favorite stories involved some sort of wisdom imparted by the cabbie during an honest talk about love, family or work.

The stereotype of the "cabbie philosopher" has infiltrated modern consciousness, much like that of the sympathetic bartender. According to Graham Russell Gao Hodges' book, *Taxi! A Social History of the New York City Cabdriver*, this archetype crystallized during the Great Depression, when educated men, like professors and engineers, lost their jobs and tried to make a living as hacks.

The modern incarnation of the cabbie philosopher operates in many ways. But in general, they listen to a passenger's story, then repackage their life experience, tie a bow around it, and offer it as advice. At this point, spiritual people who eat tempeh and burn sage while doing yoga, think, "There are no coincidences—it's fate! The spirit of the world sent me this advice!" Other people think, "Wow, what an interesting cab ride. And what lousy advice."

Just because they're known for dishing out wisdom doesn't mean cabbies don't need a dose for themselves. Sometimes, these life-altering pearls come from passengers. Drivers, like bartenders, understand it's sometimes easier to unburden one's soul to strangers.

THE KING OF THE JEWS
~

Seth Golden jokingly refers to himself as "the only Jew in New York without ambition."

He blames his parents for his lack of aspirations. When he was young, other Jewish parents in Brooklyn and Manhattan pushed their kids to achieve. They may have been poor families from Russia or Poland, but their children learned skills and Jewish culture. They studied the Torah or played violin pieces by Gustav Mahler. Most Jewish children were expected to excel. Most Jewish children would not have become taxi drivers.

But not Seth. His father never pushed him. Only once did his dad make any attempt to instill in his son what it meant to be a Jew, to show Seth his roots.

"Sit down, Seth," his father said to him.

Seth sat down. His father took out a record and put it on the record player.

"I want you to listen to this," he said. "This is your culture. These are your people."

The record was *The 2000 Year Old Man,* starring comedic icon Mel Brooks, a Brooklyn Jew born Melvin Kaminsky. The record was based on a handful of TV comedy skits performed in the early 1960s by Mel Brooks and Carl Reiner, another New York Jew. Listening to the record, Seth laughed until his sides split. He listened, fascinated, as Mel Brooks portrayed his life as a 2,000-year-old man.

After this introduction, Seth devoured all Brooks' work. He idolized the comedian, and listened to his voice as if it were from on high. He even referred to Brooks as the King of the Jews.

Over the years, Seth's lack of ambition landed him in the driver's seat of a yellow cab. One Saturday afternoon, Seth, a stocky man with a good-natured face, was driving his taxi to Manhattan from Kennedy Airport. He had just crossed over the Fifty-ninth Street Bridge, when he saw a man hustling towards the corner of Fifty-sixth Street. The man had his hand out, hoping to flag down a cab. Seth pulled over to the side, and the man walked to the curb and got in the backseat behind the driver's seat. Seth never saw his face.

Then Seth heard a familiar voice.

"I'm going to Forty-fourth and Broadway. But you can't make a left on to Broadway from Forty-fifth or Forty-seventh Streets, so you're going to have to go across earlier than that."

"Oh my God!" Seth remembered thinking. "The King of the Jews is in my cab!"

Seth had driven a slew of famous people, but he never cared to talk with them. He preferred to chat with the average guy off the street—it was a great way to pass time, and he learned a lot from his passengers. But this time was different. This was Mel Brooks!

He began to sweat. He wanted this cab ride to be a memorable time for both of them. And like many New Yorkers accustomed to seeing celebrities, he wanted to give Brooks his space; he didn't want the ride stunted by the fact that he was a huge fan, or by what he might say.

But he just had to talk to Brooks. He decided to play it cool, hoping he wouldn't mess it up.

Seth answered him in a professional voice. "OK, I'll go across Forty-ninth Street then and turn left onto Broadway."

"Good," Brooks answered.

Seth drove to Forty-ninth Street and made a right turn. As luck would have it, traffic was backed up behind two double-parked trucks.

Brooks moved over to where Seth could see him in the rear-view mirror.

"Would you look at that!" he said, motioning to the trucks. "One to the left, one to the right. They don't care. They're getting paid by the hour. You, on the other hand, you have a tough job."

He looked at Seth.

"I can see you're not the normal cab driver."

As most New York cab drivers are immigrants with accents and darker skin, this is usually an invitation for some racist comment. It's a game Seth doesn't enjoy. Sometimes passengers say to him, "Oh, a white driver!" to which he replies, "Oh, I'm not white," pausing to make them nervous before saying, "I'm Jewish." Other times, people will say, "Oh, an American driver!" His retort to this is, "No, I'm not American. I'm from Brooklyn."

Seth thought for a second. He wanted to engage Brooks. He needed to play his cards right.

"Well, I was born in Brooklyn, grew up in Brooklyn and Queens, and I live in Manhattan in a rent-stabilized apartment."

"Beautiful!" Brooks said. "I bet you're paying less than a thousand dollars a month."

"Well, I am!"

His plan had worked, thanks to his wife's apartment. When Seth and Margaret got together, he left the outer boroughs and became the envy of his friends by moving into Margaret's rent-stabilized place on Washington Square Park.

"Oh, that's great," Brooks said.

After this bit of nudging, Brooks was off to the races.

"You know," he shared, "I was born in Brooklyn, too, in Williamsburg, and my first apartment right after World War II was in the Village, on Horatio Street and West Fourth."

"Really?" Seth said.

"Yes, I had to share a bathroom, but oh, it was great," Brooks said. "I was in the Village, I was happy, I was twenty-one years old. Things were just great."

"Really," Seth said, keeping the conversation moving. "Did you live in the Village a long time?"

"Yeah, well, I then got a second apartment on Bank Street, and this is what I consider my best apartment ever," he said. "You see, I'm a writer, and I was starting to make pretty good money, and I was going out every night. I was going to jazz clubs and restaurants, and, you know, just having the greatest time of my life. But I made a big mistake."

"What's that?" Seth asked, amazed that Brooks just introduced himself as a writer—as if he hadn't inhaled everything he could read by Brooks.

"I moved to the Upper West Side," Brooks said.

"What's wrong with that?"

"Oh, you know, everything's in the Village," he explained. "It was good to me. I kept going down to the Village. I missed it."

Seth couldn't believe it. He was conversing with the King of the Jews.

"Well, you know, it's not that far," Seth said.

"Yeah, I know, but it wasn't the same. But I met my wife there. Then we moved to California. We can't complain. We lived a few blocks from the beach in Santa Monica. I've got a kid, a rotten kid, who kicked me out of his apartment. I'm not too happy with him."

Seth was taking it all in and just driving. He knew very well who Mel Brooks' wife was—the actress Anne Bancroft, who Seth fondly remembered in her role as sultry Mrs. Robinson in *The Graduate*.

Seth knew that Anne Bancroft grew up in the Bronx in an Italian family, and that her given name was Anna Maria Louisa Italiano. He had also heard that Brooks' mother wasn't originally happy with his choice in a partner. Allegedly, when Brooks told his mother he was marrying an Italian, she said, "Bring her over. I'll be in the kitchen with my head in the oven."

Like Brooks, Seth had married outside of the Jewish clan— Margaret's family came to New York from Ireland. Seth's mom was none too pleased with an Irish daughter-in-law. "Well, at least she's white," she said.

It wasn't only Seth's mother who worried about him marrying outside the clan. Seth's friend, Mike, had married a religious Jewish woman named Helen. She wasn't religious in the Orthodox sense, but in the sense that being Jewish was very important to her. When Seth first started dating Margaret, she and Helen met at a party. There, Helen took her aside and asked, "Are you two thinking of having children?"

"We don't know, we'll see how it goes," Margaret answered.

"Well, you know, if you have children, they'll be nothing," Helen said, referring to the Jewish belief that their religion is passed down to the children through the mother.

If Seth had children with a Catholic woman, they wouldn't be Jewish in the purest sense, making them "nothing." But Seth and Margaret didn't let such attitudes bother them.

Seth continued prying information from Brooks. He never let on that he knew about Brooks' wife and family. He didn't want Brooks to clam up. He kept his cool.

"You liked California, though, huh?"

"Well, you know, it was a few blocks from the beach," he said. "It's not New York, but I can't complain."

Seth played up the Jewish angle.

"Well, can you get a good piece of pastrami there?" he asked.

"Well," Brooks answered thoughtfully. "It's not like it's from Vilnius, but it's not bad."

"You know what gets me?" Brooks continued. "The bagels out there, they have no bite to them. You take a bite and they just collapse. They got no bite! I could never get used to that. Terrible bagels out in California."

Seth made his move. He turned around and looked him in the eye.

"Listen. What do the *goyim* care about food," he said slowly.

Brooks looked at him, eyes wide, as if Seth had some supreme knowledge. He was impressed.

"You're absolutely right!" he said. "Give them tuna and toast and they're happy."

At that point, it took all of Seth's will power not to pull the cab over, jump into the back seat and give Brooks a big kiss on the lips. He just couldn't believe it—he was schticking with the King of the Jews. It was just too much.

And then the ultimate moment for Seth came. Brooks said, almost sheepishly, "You know, I got a play on Broadway, *The Producers*, have you seen it?"

As if Seth—or anyone else in New York—hadn't heard of *The Producers*. The musical had been open for two months and was an instant sensation. It was impossible to get tickets. Brooks would receive three Tony Awards for the show in the 2001.

Although Brooks had revealed his identity, Seth wasn't ready to reveal himself as Brooks' biggest fan, just in case his idol would crawl back into his shell.

"No, I haven't seen it," he said. "How's that going?"

"It's going great," Brooks said with enthusiasm. "We didn't know what we had. I'm very happy with the director and the actors. But, you know, a great play can close in two days, and a bad play can go on forever. You just never know what you have on Broadway. But we've been lucky. And people are coming to see it, and it's working out great."

"Oh, that's good," answered Seth noncommittally. "You have a hit Broadway play."

Seth paused for a moment, then said, "What about making *Young Frankenstein* into a Broadway musical?"

"Well, it would require a lot of work," Brooks replied, thoughtfully. "I'd have to write a lot of songs for that. You know, for *The Producers* we had a few songs in place. I had to write a few songs, but that was really much easier. *Young Frankenstein*, well, I don't know, that would be very difficult, but we'll see."

"I think that would be good idea." Seth said to him. (Today, it's not lost on Seth that Brooks turned *Young Frankenstein* into a musical).

Seth drove in silence for a short while.

Then Brooks asked, in the same quiet voice, "Are you happy doing this? Is this enough for you? Driving a taxi?"

Seth had tried a stint teaching English to junior high kids in the Bronx. He quit in part because the money wasn't there. Also, he missed the cab and the energy of actively being part of the city. But he didn't feel like going into it. He turned around to Brooks.

"Well, I'm doing the best I can here. I'm paying my bills," he answered. "Are you happy? Are you happy writing hit musicals? How are things going for you?"

"Well, I can't complain," Brooks said.

"Well I can't complain, either," Seth replied.

Seth pulled up across the street from the St. James Theater, home to *The Producers.*

"It's $6.10 please," he said. Brooks paid him, giving him a handsome tip. Seth wasn't quite ready to let him go.

"Listen, do you want a receipt?" he asked.

"I'm rich, I don't need receipts," Brooks said.

"Really?"

Brooks put his hand out, and shook Seth's hand.

"Let me ask you something," Seth said. "You know, like you, I married *goyim.*"

Brooks gave him a look, surprised that he knew this fact.

"Good," Brooks said. "*Goyim* are good. Stick with the *goyim.*"

And he got out of the cab.

When Seth got home that evening, he had an important phone call to make. He called his friend Mike, who also idolized Brooks, and told him the story. Then he asked to speak with Mike's wife, Helen.

Helen picked up the line.

"Helen, how are you?" Seth asked. "Listen, I had Mel Brooks in the cab today, you know, the King of the Jews."

"Really?" Helen replied. "Wow, how was that?"

"Oh, it was great," Seth said. "You know, he's the funniest man alive. I was like a straight man for Mel Brooks, I made him laugh. It was great. But a curious thing happened at the end of the ride. You know, he's married to Ann Bancroft and she's Catholic. Italian, not Jewish. So I asked the King of the Jews, 'like you I married *goyim.*' And you know what he said?"

"What?" Helen asked.

"Mel Brooks said, 'Good. *Goyim* are good. Stick with the *goyim.*"

"Really?" Helen said.

"Yeah. Do you remember a few years ago, when we were at a party, and you asked Margaret about having children? She said she wasn't sure, and you said that if we had kids, they'd be nothing?"

Silence followed.

"I don't know," Helen said quietly. "Did I say that? I don't remember."

"It's not very important, but I wanted to tell you that the King of the Jews has sanctioned our marriage," Seth said. "So whatever happens here has been sanctioned by the King, so any rabbi or anybody else that comes along and says it's 'nothing,' they don't matter. I have the King on my side."

CALLING IN SICK

~

After bolting out of a bar to get away from a boring first date, Rebecca Donner stood on the cold street, trying to hail a cab. There was nothing wrong with her blind date. On paper he looked great. A tall, attractive Swede with high cheekbones and a PhD in applied physics, she had met him through the online dating site Nerve. com. Tonight had been their first face-to-face date. They met in an intimate wine bar with low lighting and exposed brick walls. The setting was perfect for romance, but once she spoke with him, Rebecca knew immediately there was no chemistry. She sucked it up and toiled through the conversation, drinking two glasses of wine.

The waiter hadn't even dropped off the check before she interrupted her date in mid-conversation, saying, "I'm sorry, I have to get up early tomorrow."

She made to leave, taking her wallet out of her purse to put money on the table. He insisted on paying.

"Thanks," she said, putting her money away. She stood up, put on her jean jacket, said good-bye, and then left, knowing how lame her excuse sounded.

She was thinking of the boring date as she climbed in the cab near Washington and Eleventh. At her request, the cabbie drove east towards her apartment in Alphabet City. Her thoughts turned to the guy she had been dating for the past two months. He wasn't boring. If anything, he kept her too much on her toes. But she liked that. He wanted a committed relationship, but Rebecca, freshly divorced, wasn't sure she was ready.

The cabbie looked in his rear-view mirror.

"How was your evening?" he asked. He was stocky, spoke with an accent, and had warm brown eyes.

"Fine," Rebecca answered noncommittally.

Her long, wavy blond hair always attracted attention, and cab drivers often tried to initiate conversation. Tonight, she preferred to sit in the back seat alone with her thoughts about the date and how dull it had been. Why had she even bothered going out with him in the first place?

After a few minutes, the driver tried again.

"So, your evening was fine?" he pressed.

This time she answered honestly.

"I had a bad date."

"Oh, a real jerk, huh?" he asked.

"No," she responded. "He was a nice guy, I just wasn't interested in him in the slightest."

She went on to tell him about the guy she was dating, how fascinating he was, and why she really liked him.

"I have eight sisters and four daughters, so there are a lot of women in my life—I know women," the cab driver said. "If you don't want to date other people, if you don't feel that you're interested in dating other people, then you know you love this man. And if you love this man, you need to tell him. And you need to tell him that you are not interested in dating other men."

He continued talking, saying that if Rebecca and the guy she was dating were mentally compatible, and if they were good friends and were attracted to each other physically, they could have a chance at long-term happiness.

Rebecca raised her eyebrows. Listening intently, she wasn't sure whether to look at his profile or at his eyes reflected by the rearview mirror. She decided to keep looking at the mirror.

The cabbie met her gaze in the rearview mirror, and raised a forefinger before making his next point.

"You must lie just a little bit in the beginning," he said. "You must pretend that you are sick. See how he reacts—whether he tries to take care of you. And if he does, you know he is a good man."

Rebecca didn't share this with the driver, but a couple weeks before she had gotten a Brazilian bikini wax. When she and her guy went to bed, she couldn't sleep because she was sore and swollen. When her guy asked why she was fussing, she answered. Although he was well on his way to sleep, he told her to get some paper towels, soak them in cold water, bring them back to bed and use them as a compress. She followed his advice, and felt better. Did this count as him taking care of her when she was sick, she wondered?

Her driver continued talking about women. He told Rebecca about how he had slept with dozens of women when he was young and still living in Romania. He shared the story of how he met his wife, how he knew that he loved her and how he didn't want any other women. About how his wife didn't trust him at first, calling him a womanizer, and about how he thought she might just be with him for his American green card. But they learned to trust each other and were meant for each other.

"I love women," he said. "I can still say, look what a beautiful ass, such a nice figure. I'm not blind! Please. But I don't touch. I love my wife and I must always be faithful to her."

He pulled up to Rebecca's apartment building, and fixed his penetrating gaze into the rear-view mirror again.

"So if you know you love this man, you must tell him and tell him soon. Don't waste your time on other men."

"Thank you very much," Rebecca said, and tried to give him a 30 percent tip on the fare.

He went to give her change.

"No, that's all for you," she said. "Thank you very much for your advice."

He took the money, but wanted to make sure Rebecca took his advice.

"OK, OK, but tell him soon!" he said. "You must have this conversation face-to-face. Look into his eyes and say what is in your heart."

Rebecca got out of the cab, and walked the six flights of steps up to her one-bedroom apartment. She got out her cell phone, and called her guy.

"We need to have a conversation, but we need to have it face-to-face," she said.

Then she sneezed loudly.

"Are you all right?" he asked.

"I think I'm coming down with a cold," she lied.

PLAYING IT FORWARD

~

The press intern responsible for Lincoln Center's free outdoor concerts, Lauren Weiner, was on the verge of collapse. It was the middle of the July 2001 heat wave, and she had been standing outside under the beating sun since the 9 a.m. sound check. She stayed outside through the afternoon concert, breathing air so thick with humidity that she wanted to grow gills. It seemed like she dealt with thousands of cranky journalists and musicians.

Finally, the evening show began. Lauren sat backstage listening to the music. When the musicians wrapped up at 11 p.m., she grabbed her tote-bag like purse, which had been stashed under a chair for hours, and bolted away to hail a cab before anyone could ask her for anything else.

"I'm going to Forty-third and Eleventh Avenue," Lauren said.

The trip only took five minutes. The driver pulled into the circular driveway in front of her building, and Lauren reached into her purse for her wallet.

She found her cell phone, keys, water bottle and press folders, but couldn't find her wallet.

"It has to be here somewhere," she mumbled under her breath while she fished around.

It wasn't. Tired, hot, and thirsty, she started to cry.

"I'm so sorry," she told the driver, her voice wavering. "My wallet is missing."

"Calm down," the driver said.

His voice reassured her with its fatherly tone. He dark eyes looked at her through the rearview mirror.

"Where did you last see it?"

"I don't know. I think it's been stolen! I left my purse under a chair for hours with no one around."

"Just in case, where did you last see it," he said patiently.

Lauren noticed his accent, but was too tired and overwrought to figure out where he was from—South Asia or the Middle East was her best guess.

She mentally retraced her steps through the day and remembered the few hours she spent that afternoon in her air-conditioned office.

"My office, I guess. If it's not stolen, the only place it can be is my office," she said.

"And where's your office?"

"Where you picked me up. Lincoln Center."

She wiped the tears off her face with her hand.

"I'll take you back to Lincoln Center and you can look in your office."

"Okay," she said in a small voice.

The ride back to Lincoln Center only took a few minutes. The cabbie double-parked by the escalator.

"I'll wait outside for you," he said.

"You know, I don't know if I'll find my wallet," Lauren said. "And if I don't find my wallet, I don't know if I can pay you."

"Don't worry," he said. "I'll wait."

She ran into the building, signed in, and waited impatiently for the elevator. The cabbie's attitude made her nervous. A long-time New Yorker, she wasn't sure if he was being generous or was gunning for an inappropriately large tip.

She got out of the elevator, ran to her office, and looked under her desk. The wallet was there, on the floor. She picked it up and looked inside it. Everything was still there—her driver's license, credit cards and about thirty dollars in cash.

She went back downstairs, out the front door, and saw the driver waiting. She smiled at him.

"I found my wallet!" she said as she got back into the cab.

"Good, I'm glad," he said in his fatherly way.

On the way back to her apartment, Lauren called her roommate, who was at work, to tell her what happened. It wasn't until they pulled into her driveway that Lauren realized the meter was off.

"How much do I owe you?" she asked.

"Nothing," he said.

Lauren tried to estimate how much three trips to and from Lincoln Center would cost and took that much out of her purse.

"Take it, really," she said.

He waved her money away.

"Nothing," he repeated. "Just do something nice for someone."

"Of course," said Lauren, genuinely touched.

She opened up her wallet, took out all thirty dollars.

"No," he said, waving her hand away, smiling. "I'm just happy it worked out."

These days, Lauren consistently over-tips anyone who works in the service industry, especially taxi drivers.

CREDIT CHECK

~

In 2008, the average cab driver works nine or nine and a half hours a day. And having credit card machines have been good for cabbies' business.

Now that every cab has a credit card reader and a computerized system—new since November 2008—the TLC has plenty of new information on taxi trips and fares. For example, cabs are busiest between 6 and 8 p.m.

While drivers vigorously opposed the addition of the credit card machine—they personally pay a five percent transaction processing fee—it seems customers' plastic habits has kept the taxi industry afloat during the recession, according to the TLC.

One serious downside of the new system: The credit card reader is attached to a TV, meaning passengers and drivers alike are assaulted by advertising and programming that automatically comes on when the cab takes off.

HARLEM IN MIND

~

Graham Russell Hodges drove his cab wearing an old, leather coat, a tank top, velvet shorts and plastic sandals. It was 1974, he was twenty-seven years old, and he felt the bohemian look suited him. An American studies graduate student living in the East Village, Graham felt his dress effectively communicated his creativity, his need for attention, and his anger at the establishment.

He battled his way uptown through the flow of taxis and buses. Just beyond Seventy-Second Street and Madison, a group of people hailed him. A pudgy white man in an expensive suit and with a pricey haircut slid into the front seat. Three people got into the back: a younger white man, a tall slim black woman in her twenties with a pretty face, and a corpulent older black man who looked to be in his eighties. The older man took up much of the back seat because of his girth and height. At six-foot-three, he stood as tall as Graham.

"We're heading to Elaine's," said the man sitting up front. Graham had driven other clients to the Upper East Side restaurant, a staple hangout for New York's most famous literary, film and theater stars. He wondered who his passengers were.

Graham drove towards the restaurant while the man beside him flipped through a book of photography. Graham kept looking over his shoulder, trying to get a better look at the pictures. He could see they were images of African Americans, but that was it.

He couldn't contain himself. "What are those photos of?" he finally asked.

The man nodded his head towards the backseat. "The photographer is in the cab. It's James Van Der Zee."

Graham had never heard of James Van Der Zee. He looked at the man again through the rearview mirror. He wore a suit and conveyed an air of formality without looking like he wanted to impress. Graham turned back to the photos in the other man's lap.

A light turned red and Graham braked. Noticing his interest in the pictures, the guy in the front seat said, "Would you like to look?"

"Sure," said Graham, and he reached over for the book.

The photos were of African Americans in the 1920s and 1930s. None of his photos portrayed downtrodden or isolated blacks—these were wedding portraits, family photos, and shots of church groups or parades marching up the street. The composition was well-conceived, but it was the content Graham found extraordinary. He had never seen photos of middle class blacks before.

The man explained each picture as they flipped through the book.

"This is of Marcus Garvey," he said, although Graham immediately recognized the famous black nationalist leader.

The photos took Graham through a tour of Harlem's streets. They captured famous jazz performers, beautiful women in hats and dresses and children playing.

It seemed logical to Graham that the older man in his backseat took the photos. He was the only one of the three alive during that period. Graham saw Van Der Zee had an extraordinary understanding of urban life in New York, something Graham, the son of a minister and nurse-turned-homemaker from upstate New York, admired.

Graham wanted to learn more about the photos' subjects. He had recently become interested in African-American culture, and had been reading about the civil rights movement. Graham was also becoming more aware of history on a deeper level. He knew that in the early 1900s, the years portrayed in the photos, southern blacks took part in the Great Migration, moving northwards and away from the segregated south. It was the age of the Harlem Renaissance, when black literature, art and music flourished against a backdrop of racial unrest.

Graham flipped through the photos at every red light. His excitement became infectious, and the man beside him smiled more easily and talked more. When they reached Elaine's, where the group had reservations to celebrate the release of Van Der Zee's book, the man asked Graham, "Would you like to come in and eat with us?"

Graham couldn't tell if the invitation was just friendly or sexual, but he really didn't care. He wanted to learn more about Van Der Zee.

"Sure," he said.

The young woman got out and helped Van Der Zee, who walked with a cane. Together they went into Elaine's, Graham wearing his plastic sandals.

The hostess sat the ten people in Van Der Zee's party at a long table in a back room. Graham quickly became aware that the publisher/gallery owner was not happy with his presence, and that it was this man's assistant who had sat next to Graham and extended the invitation. Graham talked a bit to everyone, but mostly he kept his mouth shut. He knew he wasn't the guest of honor. Also, he couldn't join in the conversations about Van Der Zee's photographs because he didn't know them well.

NATIVE SONS

~

A white taxi driver with a New York accent is as rare as coconuts in Canada. In other words, a figment of the imagination.

Anyone studying cabbies' ethnicities may as well memorize a United Nations fact book. In 2006, 91 percent of cab drivers were born in foreign countries, according to Schaller Consulting. Nearly half of immigrant cab drivers arrived from Pakistan, Bangladesh or India, which explains the number of taxis parked outside Manhattan's South Asian food joints. Haitians, Egyptians and citizens of the former Soviet Union also make up a large chunk of drivers. Rising numbers of cabbies from Morocco, Nigeria and Ghana reflect New York's increasing African population.

As recently as 1984, 26 percent of hack license applicants were born in the U.S. The change reflects New York's immigration patterns, although many American-born cabbies say the implementation of the leasing system—where cabbies pay a fee to rent cabs rather than share profits with their garages—pushed American drivers towards more secure jobs and opened the door for immigrants.

But listening in on the conversations around him, Graham learned more about Van Der Zee. The man had been a distinguished cameraman in Harlem for decades, and he had a number of photography books out. He had recently been rediscovered, and the photographer generated an international following when he was featured in the Metropolitan Museum of Art exhibit, "Harlem on my Mind."

People considered his work unmatchable as a social record of this period of black life as well as technically precise. He also learned that the young woman in the cab was Van Der Zee's wife.

Graham paid Van Der Zee a number of compliments, which the man accepted, but on the whole Van Der Zee ignored him. Graham knew he was out of place, but stayed because he'd been invited. He ate the food, drank the wine, studied the people, and was the first to leave.

The next day, Graham bought the famous photographer's new book plus several others featuring his work. From the books he learned that Van Der Zee started taking pictures in his hometown of Lenox, Massachusetts. He moved to Harlem in 1906 at age nineteen, and a number of years and odd jobs later, opened his own photography studio. He became locally famous for his portraits.

Van Der Zee wanted Harlem to look its best. He filled in bald spots, retouched crooked teeth, and painted on jewelry. He dramatically posed his subjects to tell a story, such as having parents listening to their children playing piano. He used backdrops, costumes, and sophisticated lighting, adding elements of glamour. He even created photo montages, or many images in one picture, one of which showed the superimposed image of a girl floating above her casket. He photographed all of Harlem, from the most famous to the least.

As with the rest of Harlem, Van Der Zee's fortunes fell after World War II. He and his wife were destitute when he was rediscovered in 1968 by a representative from the Metropolitan Museum doing research for the "Harlem on My Mind" exhibit.

Armed with his new-found knowledge, Graham went through a phone book and found the listing for Van Der Zee, James. He dialed the number. Once a collector of signed baseball cards, Graham had since become a collector of signed books. He hoped Van Der Zee would sign his for him.

Van Der Zee's wife, Donna, answered the phone. She vaguely remembered Graham.

"I really enjoyed meeting Mr. Van Der Zee, I've bought some of his books, and I'd like to come up and visit for a couple of minutes and have him sign them," Graham told her. "I will not be intrusive."

She somewhat reluctantly invited him to stop by.

A few days later, Graham parked his cab and visited their home just off Central Park West. The Van Der Zees seemed surprised to hear from him, but they invited him up.

Their apartment seemed ordinary, except for the stacks of boxes. The couple had several aged cats, one of which had cancerous tumors on its back. Van Der Zee didn't look that much better. His massive body seemed to collapse, and his wife had to help him walk. But he signed Graham's books and sold him a limited edition of the book, *The Harlem Book of the Dead*. During their brief conversation, Van Der Zee mentioned that he was thinking of getting a new apartment with better light to restart his business. Graham wondered why he would bother, given the man's old age, but he held his tongue. A few minutes later, Graham went back to his cab with the autographed copies under his arm.

One year after visiting the Van Der Zees apartment, Graham received a flyer in the mail promoting Van Der Zee's new gallery show. Graham went to the opening, and as he walked through the door, Van Der Zee spotted him and chuckled. "The cab driver!"

"Go look at my new stuff," he said, still laughing.

Graham walked around the gallery, taking in the portraits of famous African Americans like Bill Cosby, Diana Ross and Sidney Poitier. The old man had done it. He re-launched his career when he was in his eighties. Celebrities jumped to have their photographs taken by him; they paid thousands of dollars apiece for the privilege.

As Graham left the gallery, he told Van Der Zee how much he liked the portraits.

He felt ashamed that a year ago he almost told the old man to give up and unpack his boxes. It would be Van Der Zee's late-in-life drive that would help Graham reshape his vision of his own future.

Over the years, Van Der Zee's books became some of Graham's most treasured possessions. He began moving closer to Van Der Zee's world and the urban minority lifestyle, and Van Der Zee's books gave him a better understanding of African Americans.

Graham earned his doctorate in history, became a professor at Colgate University and a leading scholar of African-American history in and around New York. His experience with Van Der Zee was one of many that prompted Graham to write his book, *Taxi! A Social History of the New York City Cabdriver*.

Many historians do their best work into their sixties and seventies. Graham, or Professor Hodges, as his students call him, hopes to do the same, but even later in life. After all, his idols—Van Der Zee is one—created well into their eighties.

CHAPTER 5

CABBIE OVERACHIEVERS
When the Meter's Not Running

Every taxi driver has a deeper story than the one frantic episode showcased in this book. Simply the fact that 90 percent of cab drivers were born in foreign countries means most have stories of coming to the United States. Maybe they were simply sponsored by an uncle in Brooklyn. Or maybe they traveled across a desert on camel before stowing away on a cargo ship, hiding in burlap bags as rats nibbled their toes.

Either way, it takes a certain kind of person to leave their family, their rituals and their way of life and move to a foreign country, where, chances are, they'll spend the next few years making embarrassing cultural gaffes and mispronouncing English. Those who had careers as engineers or literature professors in their country know their education and skills will count for little, if anything, in America.

All this suggests, albeit in a highly unscientific way, that many New York cab drivers are risk takers and adventurers, in the sense that they'll give up the familiar for a taste of something different, and, hopefully, better. Even those who moved to the United States only to send money to their family across the world took that risk. At least once, they jumped at change and perceived opportunity.

The story of drivers' arrival in New York and their journey to master the yellow cab paints only part of their individual pictures. When it came to choosing cabbies for profiles, I sought out drivers who, when they looked at their taxi, saw more than a hunk of metal with four doors and a gas-guzzling tank. Instead, they saw creative possibilities. One driver, who dreamed of photographing people on New York's streets, achieved fame for the pictures he snapped of his passengers. Another uses his cab to spread the word about his charity, founded to help impoverished children in his homeland, India.

Ultimately, you have no idea who's behind the wheel. They could be a former microbiologist and author, or a talented matchmaker. Or they could be the village idiot who won the green card lottery. But one thing you can almost always count on: Most cabbies have stellar hand-eye coordination, allowing them to successfully navigate New York's traffic. That may not make them profile-worthy, but it does help with getting people home in one piece.

NEVER GOING ALONG, NEVER GOT ALONG

~

Ryan Weideman moved to NYC in 1980, hoping to become a famous street photographer. But his twelve-hour shifts as a cab driver barely allowed him time on the streets—at least outside of a rolling vehicle. One day, Ryan strapped his camera onto his cab's sun visor with two rubber bands. When his next customer stepped into the cab, he said, "Hi, I'm a photographer, and I'd like to take your picture."

The cab became Ryan's studio, if not his muse. He shot arresting black and white images, capturing the laughter of pierced punks, the reserve and hauteur of the upper crust, the exhaustion of hooker transvestites. Some photos included Ryan's angular face and unblinking gaze along with his passengers, bringing together the often separate worlds of cab drivers and their clients. The photos found an audience and Ryan made a name for himself. Chelsea's Bruce Silverstein Gallery held exhibits featuring his work, and he had a piece auctioned off by Sotheby's. A handful of his photographs belong in the permanent collections of museums.

A tall, lanky man with a beatnik air, the sixty-six-year-old Ryan says that while he asked passengers if he could take their photos, he didn't necessarily obey their requests.

"Some people say no, but I do it anyway," drawls Ryan, his voice molasses-slow and even, leaving plenty of space between each word.

"Some have threatened to hit me with their purses. Some have actually hit me."

He pauses for effect. The long fingers of one hand forms the shape of a gun.

"I have an itchy trigger finger. No control."

The photos rarely feel anonymous. Instead, they feel like a moment Ryan shared with his passengers. You sense his camaraderie for the traditional societal outcasts in his cab, and you sense that he wanted to participate in many of these people's lives.

"It's lonely in the front of a cab," he said. "I wanted to be in the back where the action was. I wanted to meet girls. Maybe crawl in the back seat."

Pause.

"Just kidding."

Sometimes he would take part in his passengers' lives, joining them for an evening out, parking his cab and taking his cameras into clubs and parties.

"My favorite moment is when they invite you in," he said. "I'm about the human connection."

He set up rules for hanging out with passengers. For example, he would go to parties, but not into their homes. While Ryan made it clear that he passed up a number of opportunities with the ladies, it has been said that he's dated women he met in his cab. When pressed to talk about it, his eyes become two dark points of anger. Instead of answering, he changes the topic and pontificates about driving, using expressions like, "squeeze through double-parked cars like toothpaste," and "burrow through the city like a rat."

When it came to hunting for fares, Ryan followed the action. He joined lines of cabs waiting for passengers outside the Mudd Club and other hot venues. One night, after the first couple of cabs in line turned down a group of eight punk rockers (they refused to risk so many people in their taxis), Ryan waved the group over and told them to get in. After all, he drove the old Checker cab with a spacious back seat and a couple extra seats that flipped down.

"Hey you guys," he said. "I'm a photographer, and I'm going to photograph you guys."

The group played it up, posing and performing for Ryan, each trying to outdo the other. Their after-party location was a burnt-out abandoned building on the Lower East Side. Ryan accompanied them into the party for a few hours. Then he went home and developed his photos.

He also shot a photo of himself driving Alan Ginsburg. In the photo, Ryan's unsmiling face stares straight ahead, while Ginsburg, holding up a piece of paper, looks jolly and affable.

Invisible to the naked eye is the poem Ginsburg wrote on the paper, "Backseat of a New York Taxi is a human zoo. Ryan Weideman taxi-dermist has mounted these human species types with humor and boldness and precision. A passenger Allen Ginsberg 12/2/90."

Although he has lived in New York for more than twenty-seven years and he made a name for himself photographing the city in the 1980s, Ryan doesn't consider New York his home.

"No one likes me. Not even New York likes me. Yosemite is my home. Those mountains are my home. That's where I belong."

Driving a cab gives Ryan a flexible schedule, and every year he takes off August, September and October and heads into nature out West. Like most New Yorkers, he needs to get out of the city.

At first reluctant to share his personal history, when pushed, Ryan said he came from California, although he later admitted to being born in the Midwest, the son of German-American farmers from Oklahoma. He believed driving was in his blood. His father had a 1939 Ford, and would sit behind the steering wheel and tear down the open road. His dad always said he wanted to drive in a Mexican road race. Ryan calls himself a street demon. Look at the end of his last name, he says. It's "deman," like demon.

Ryan grimaces when asked for more details about his past.

"Never going along, never get along," he says. "It's just my natural way."

Once the stories of his life are pieced together, this expression sounds like his mantra.

Ryan's Midwest is one of dust-torn plains and hard lives. His father lost the farm during the Great Depression when Ryan was one-and-a-half years old. Some of Ryan's earliest memories come to life in black and white photos taken when the farm was auctioned off, photographs that would fit in a Walker Evans montage.

"*Grapes of Wrath* style," he says. "He was angry and took it out on everyone. I kind of understand now. My father looked at me and, no matter what, my life was easier. It really broke his heart when he lost the farm."

The family moved to Kansas, where his father got a job and Ryan got in trouble. By the age of sixteen, he found himself in cell block nine. Ryan refuses to say why he was on the wrong side of the law.

"I'd rather not talk about it," he said with finality.

Instead, he talks about how he wracked his brains for a possible alternative to prison.

The next day, he stood before the Kansas judge and asked him to ship him to a farm in Oklahoma instead of sending him to jail. The judge agreed and, like a character from a western, gave him until sundown to get out of town.

Ryan memorized the drive to Oklahoma in photographic frames. The dark night, the rain, the car slipping all over the road. His father cursing the entire way. The plains of Oklahoma opening up before him. They went to his grandparents' house in the heart of the wide open, spooky land. He asked if he could live with his aunt, her husband, and their kids. They agreed, so he lived with them and worked on their farm for a year.

His father took to calling him "desperado," but Ryan was proud that his problems gave him an opportunity to live off the land like his ancestors. He liked waking up at 3 or 4 a.m. to feed and care for the animals and to milk the cows.

When he turned eighteen, Ryan returned to Kansas where he promptly "got into trouble" again. This time he joined the military to avoid jail time. When mentioned that the marines hardly seems like a place for someone who flouts authority, he gives a low whistle.

"Got into trouble there. That was big," he said. "Got out of that scrape, too."

After the armed services, he attended the California College of Arts and Crafts and earned a graduate degree in photography and printmaking. When he graduated he worked odd jobs in California, like painting fences while listening to salsa music, before trying his hand in New York.

When he went east to New York, he took a month to find an apartment he could afford, moved in and immediately set up his darkroom. He only had one thousand dollars and no job prospects. His neighbor across the hall drove a cab. Ryan needed money, so he decided to drive a cab, too. He started working days, but the congested city traffic drove him crazy. He switched to nights.

Twenty-seven years later, Ryan drives only two days a week, and he's back to driving days. He feels he found his natural schedule, going to bed at 9 or 10 p.m. and waking up before the sun rises.

"Driving nights goes against the grain of my nature," he said. "I'm a farm boy at heart."

Also, he added, dawn has the best light for taking pictures.

He no longer rubber bands a camera to his sun visor. His latest project involves driving around the United States and snapping portraits of cab drivers in cities across the country. He simply walks into local cab agencies, introduces himself, and sets up his camera. Most drivers seem to enjoy the opportunity of being documented. Some smile for the photos; most don't. The black and white photos capture every wrinkle, a slight downturn of the mouth, laughing eyes. He hopes someday to have them published in a book.

Taking photos of America's cabbies is a solid excuse to get out of New York and explore the rest of the country. He plans Detroit as one of his next stops. He's heard it's a dangerous city and imagines lots of deviants live there. Perhaps some of them are cab drivers. He would like that.

FROM IRON CURTAIN TO YELLOW CAB

~

Taxi driver Iva Pekárková calls herself lazy. When she arrived in the United States she was horrified at the average vacation allotment of ten days each year. She specifically sought out jobs that gave her more time off. After escaping the Iron Curtain of her native Czechoslovakia by walking across the border from Yugoslavia to Italy, she had a right to call her own shots.

Besides, she had a book to write. And if she couldn't get some time off, it just wasn't going to happen.

After escaping the Eastern Block, Iva lived in a refugee camp in Austria, where she toiled as a maid, a factory worker and a construction worker. She turned her back on her trained profession of microbiologist. Microbiology, she said, was sophisticated cooking, and Iva didn't cook. She got her American visa and she bored herself to tears working in a Boston lab. After arriving in New York, she tried to find inspiration in waitressing, limo driving and bartending. Iva even served as a social worker in the Bronx for a stint.

She hated all the jobs, and the mind-numbingly robotic nature of the work.

Her brain needed more stimulation. She was smart enough that Czechoslovakia's communist officials were forced to allow her to attend college. The university accepted her despite the fact that Iva's parents abandoned the party, consequently forfeiting Iva's right to an education. But Iva had simply won too many math and science contests to ignore.

Searching for a better job in New York, Iva settled on driving a taxi. It wasn't the romantic notion of driving a cab that she fell for. She knew the job entailed twelve-hour days, but it was the ability to take time off whenever she wanted, for herself and for her novels. "This is the freedom I really love," she said.

Iva isn't as lazy as she claims.

It was 1990 and Iva just turned twenty-seven. She didn't yet know that her career as cabbie would be the key to her most widely acclaimed novel, *Gimme the Money*—a best seller in the Czech Republic that would make her famous there.

Gimme the Money, published in 2000, is Iva's love story about New York as seen through the eyes of a female Czech cab driver, Gin. It's semi-autobiographical in the sense that Iva incorporated her vast and varying experiences in the city as a cabbie. She describes how old Upper East Side ladies hail cabs with their left arm, as they hold leashes for lapdogs in their right. She talks about hookers who swear their johns don't smell as bad at the Kentucky Fried Chicken where they used to work, and she clues us in on how cabbies, forbidden to carry weapons, keep baseball bats and sharpened Phillips screwdrivers under their seats.

She describes how cab drivers insulate themselves from the city; how the music on the radio protects them from the bustle, the scream of fire engine sirens, yelling drunks, cursing pedestrians, the whoosh of traffic, and from horn-blowing and middle-finger waving other drivers.

Through her book, its obvious Iva fell in love with New York— "the streets more than the people," she said. It was an unexpected consequence of her job, a job that took her to every corner of the city's boroughs.

"Never did I love a city half as much as I loved, and still love, New York," she said. "I fell in love with the way it looked, the way it behaved. Getting to know its rhythm, its hidden corners, every street crossing in Manhattan—well, that's something I really, truly, enjoyed."

Unlike many drivers, who were too frightened to take fares to the South Bronx or East New York, Iva took her customers anywhere at any time.

She knew it was risky. At the very least, she sometimes didn't get paid, which amounted to a cost of twenty or twenty-five dollars for long trips. She enjoyed the effusive thanks from stranded borough dwellers who found it nearly impossible to find a ride home. She eavesdropped on hookers and their pimps. She considered her forays into Harlem and the Bronx as fuel for her "decadent streak."

But the bad experiences left her shaken. She got held up three times—once at gunpoint, twice at knifepoint. One of the times, a kid riding in the back managed to reach around and unlock her door undetected. When he got out near Penn Station, he opened her door, put a gun to her stomach and said, "White mamma, I'm going to blow your mother fucking brains out! Give me all your mother-fucking money!"

"So I gave him all my motherfucking money," Iva said, before joking that the kid really needed a better education, thinking her brains were in her stomach.

Iva met plenty of other drivers who refused to drive to certain neighborhoods, and she even knew some who had never been to the Bronx. Yet they would tell how dangerous it was and how everyone in the Bronx would try and kill her. She met passengers in the 1980s and 1990s who lived on Manhattan's swank Park Avenue, who would tell her to avoid Harlem at all costs. But when Iva asked them the last time they went to Harlem, her passengers would inevitably answer, "Oh, I would never set foot there!"

"They really had no idea," she said.

Besides, Iva had already faced both figurative and literal gunmen at age twenty-five when she crossed the border to Italy in 1985. There was a difference between the gun wielders in the United States and in Europe. In New York, she chose to drive in the city's most feared neighborhoods. In communist Eastern Europe, choices were made for her. She studied microbiology because she knew she would never be permitted to study philosophy. She could only travel to East Germany, Hungary, Romania and Bulgaria.

"The reason I left was because I wanted my freedom," she said. "It was as simple as that. The revolution came four-and-a-half years later, and we had absolutely no idea that it would ever come. Some people in the West thought things were changing, but we had no idea from within. So I thought, I can choose to have my life in here without ever being able to travel or anything, or I can leave. So I decided to leave."

She pulled every string she could to secure a travel permit to Yugoslavia. When the permit came through, she packed her backpack, boarded the train and got off near the Italian border. She began walking. She walked across the rocky terrain, winding her way around olive trees and thorny shrubs. She knew where the border post was, and walked about five miles to circumnavigate it.

Iva had heard of people who had crossed, but it was a risk. You never knew. Perhaps she would be the unlucky woman to meet a border guard. Worse, she could meet a border guard willing to shoot. Armed guards killed many people here. Despite her fear, she kept going, passing terrace fields with low fences for keeping out goats. She crossed the border without incident, and walked into the nearest Italian village.

Unexpectedly, she found the freedom and flexibility she sought driving a cab. The scenery changed so quickly between New York's neighborhoods that cruising around the five boroughs felt like traveling to different lands, all while staying in one city. In *Gimme the Money*, she compares the bridges, tunnels and hidden alleyways of New York to the workings of the mind. Some argue that her co-patriot Franz Kafka—if a German-speaking Jew living among Czechs qualifies as co-patriot—portrayed the terrifying and colluded judicial system in his book, *The Trial*, as an allegory for the mind. Coincidentally, one of Iva's first garages, located in the west forties, was named the Kafka Garage.

It was at the Kafka Garage that she fell madly in love with a dispatcher.

Iva also switched garages a number of times. In doing so, she learned that dispatchers, the people who direct the flow of and the vibe of a garage, had a quality that attracted her.

"It was the way they knew about cars and life," she mused.

Also, dispatchers were nicer than other drivers.

She saw a lot of competition between the drivers, who needed a toughness to compete for customers late at night. Many worked twelve-hour shifts six or seven days a week.

"Some of these people worked too hard, too much, and had the humanity sucked away from them," she said.

They fought over the better cars, and while most drivers socialized within their ethnic groups, they rarely ventured outside.

The passengers were another group of misfits that she rubbed shoulders with.

"A cab driver I knew at the very first garage I worked for, an unsuccessful screenwriter, used to say that the stories you hear and/or observe while driving a cab are like detective novels with the first and last page torn off," Iva said.

She overheard bits of loves stories and heated arguments. She drove around pimps and their working girls, sharing a back seat. She sharpened her story-telling skills by creating her own beginnings and endings to her passenger's sagas.

While other cab drivers complained about sitting lonely and bored in the front seat, Iva couldn't get her passengers to shut up. Not that she tried. Being friendly earned her better tips than other cab drivers. Or maybe she earned better tips because she was female. Customers always asked the same questions.

"Are you scared driving at night?"

"Where did you learn English?"

"Where are you from?"

Iva called these series of questions, "small-talk interrogation."

A few customers offered her money for sex, but she laughed them away. But she did befriend one female driver who would gladly sit on her passengers' laps. She wore caked-on make-up and a tight miniskirt and earned tons more money as a hooker than a driver. The yellow cab she used as a prop to turn men on.

From the beginning, Iva suspected she'd use fodder from her taxi-driving career in a book. She wrote a couple of short stories about driving to figure out her angle. About four years into her stint, Iva began writing *Gimme the Money*. As she drove, she compiled her adventures. She kept a notebook beside her, and created a number of chapters while her taxi waited in line at night clubs for customers.

But the moment she finished writing the book, driving cabs lost most of its adventure for her. It was a disappointing consequence of recording years' worth of observations. Once again, she was working for money and nothing else. It was time for a change.

Together with her American boyfriend, in 1997 Iva moved back to the Czech Republic. They married, and when the Czech Republic became a member of the European Union, Iva moved to London. (Iva and her husband are now separated).

Today, Iva works in London as a minicab driver. It's something like New York's neighborhood car services.

"Now I see the adventure in it," she says.

She also gets plenty of time off.

SWEET CHARITY

~

Cab driver Om Dutta Sharma and his wife, Krishna, had been putting money aside for years—possibly to buy a house—when news came that Om Dutta's mother in India passed away.

Bereaved, Om Dutta traveled to his home village of Doobher Kishanpur, near New Delhi. While at a party celebrating his mother's life, a local tradition honoring those older than sixty who die, it hit Om Dutta what his money was for. A trained lawyer who believes the best gift you can give is knowledge, Om Dutta decided to create an all-girls' school in this village to honor his illiterate mother.

Om Dutta, who has reddish hair, sharp eyes, and a hint of impatience underlying his calm veneer, returned to America and set to work in achieving his goal. He and his wife already had a chunk of money set aside, but they would need more. He drove twelve- to fifteen-hour shifts. The family cut back on spending. He never took Krishna, a nurse at Bellevue Hospital, out to dinner or to a movie. They skimped on buying clothes for their sons. By American standards, the Sharma's scraped by on a middle-class income. But to the poor villagers in India, he became a wealthy benefactor.

In 1997, one year after his mother's death, Om Dutta opened the school in the two-story brick farmhouse where he grew up. He named it Ram Kali, after his mother. Since then, Om Dutta has added another building to his school, enabling him to educate more than four hundred girls from his village and neighboring villages in science, math, civics and reading.

He found teachers through newspaper ads and paid their salaries. Tailors created uniforms from blue and white gingham cloth. He paid for the students' medical checkups with money from a nearby mango orchard he owned with his brother. Om Dutta even paid for the girls' books, as their farmer parents could not easily do so. He offered classes up through the tenth grade, after which most village girls marry and have their own families.

Although India has co-ed schools, Om Dutta understood that rural villagers didn't approve of educating girls together with boys after the primary grades. But Om Dutta, who earned a law degree in India, also understood the value of education.

"All women, educated and not, have their heart they can use," he said. "But those girls getting educated today will have the capacity of using their brain as well as their heart. They will talk and they will listen."

Om Dutta talks and listens as he drives his cab through New York's streets. A "philosopher cabbie," he never installed a partition—the

The Medallion

~

Although the taxi medallion looks like a piece of tin fastened to a cab's hood, it's the essential component that makes a car a cab. A cab's medallion is to a sheriff's badge: Its application alone transforms a canary yellow four-door into a taxi. The medallion is a license from the city authorizing the car's operation within the five boroughs. It's also the car's identification mark, the number that disgruntled passengers copy down if they want to report something to the TLC.

As of 2009, 13,237 yellow cabs with medallions cruise around New York City looking for fares. (This number has rarely inched up since the number of medallions was fixed in 1937). Those who want to own a medallion quickly learn that they're hard to come by. Not only are their numbers limited, but they cost more than a four-bedroom home in most of America. In May of 2009, sales of some medallions to individuals topped half a million dollars, with the average price of a corporate medallion settling at $744,000 in June. The city occasionally sells new medallions via a silent auction involving sealed envelopes and nervous bidders. Those worried that purchasing a medallion would resign their families to a life of starvation need never fear—handily, they count as security for loans.

clear plastic divider separating the front seat from the back—knowing it would hinder his conversations with passengers about politics and the meaning of life. These conversations lead to the topic of his school, his mission, and to the handing out of his brochures to passengers.

One day a few years back, he spoke with a passenger about America's greed. He asked her if waking up, going to work, going home, eating and sleeping, day after day, month after month, year after year, only to really wake up at retirement, made a life worth living. She laughed and asked him if he was preaching. He gave her his brochure. Shortly thereafter, she called him and said she wrote for the *New York Daily News*, and that she hoped to write an article about him.

Her article hit newsstands, and other publications picked up on the heartwarming story of the well-educated cab driver and the sacrifices he made to enrich the lives of girls in his native country. The donations flowed in. A prominent businessman gave him $20,000. A woman in Dallas sent over $10,000. A school in Minnesota wanted to help.

"Everyone has a good heart, but they don't know what to do," said Om Dutta. "When they see other people doing good, they jump on in."

Om Dutta's life in America began in 1972, when he came to the United States as a tax lawyer for an Indian company. He lasted two months.

"I didn't like it at all. There were no Indians here."

He returned to India. Before he left, a friend loaned him four hundred dollars and told him to apply for a green card. He got it. Six weeks later he returned to the United States and started working as an accountant, but couldn't find any clients, as few Indians lived here. He switched to selling life insurance and ran into the same problem.

Om Dutta was still struggling two years later when his wife came over. A nurse, she immediately found work at Bellevue. But he desperately needed a better job. One day, standing in front of Macy's in bustling Harold Square, Om Dutta thought about driving a taxi. He hailed a cab, got in, and for the next thirty minutes pelted the Greek driver with questions.

The next day, Om Dutta sifted through newspaper ads and spotted one for a broker. He traveled to Queens, met with the guy, and had his hack license two days later. He drove for two years before the broker, now a good friend, told Om Dutta to buy a medallion. In 1979, it would cost him $85,000.

"How can I get that money!" Om Dutta exclaimed.

"Don't worry, just put $10,000 down," the broker said.

Om Dutta did. Now his medallion is worth close to half a million. He plans on selling the medallion when he retires. Naturally, some of the proceeds will go to the school.

In the meantime, Hollywood has discovered Om Dutta's story and is making a film about his life, called *Good Sharma*. He, his wife, and his cab make an appearance in the film.

Five percent of the film's proceeds will go to his charity and to his latest project—opening another all-girls school in an Indian village neighboring his own.

WORKING WOMEN

~

"More women should be professional drivers," says Aura Bobadilla, a driver for Williamsburg's Northside car service and a black car service in Manhattan. "It's a great job for mothers and for women."

With her bouncy curls and quick laugh, Aura, thirty-one, could be a spokeswoman for female drivers.

"I like driving, being in the car and going places," she said. "I like being outside in nature."

While most people wouldn't consider the streets of Brooklyn nature, you have to admire her enthusiasm.

There's no boss hounding her and she makes her own hours, as long as she stays organized. But the main advantage for Aura, who arrived here from the Dominican Republic in the mid-1990s, is the flexibility—a huge advantage for a woman with two boys, ages eight and ten.

"When you have kids, you have to stop for medical appointments. You have to stop if there's an emergency, if they get sick in school, if they get suspended, or if they do something wrong. You have to leave work and go pick up your child."

Aura tried different jobs. She earned a bachelors degree in psychology and has a paralegal certificate. She's worked in offices. Her job at the library wasn't bad. But she hated the morning rush of getting up early to get the kids ready, combined with the ensuing commotion because the kids were moving too slowly. Invariably, it involved hounding her children, running late, shooting over to school, dropping the kids off, and then starting her commute. She was exhausted before the day began.

"That builds up a lot of stress if you do it on a daily basis," she said.

At her office jobs, her bosses didn't like her leaving work once the day started.

"They don't want to hear people taking off an afternoon or a day because something happened with the family. Maybe once every six months, but if it happens frequently, they see that as a problem, a worker that's not productive."

With driving, she drops her kids off at school, and starts work that second. Virtually stress-free.

Her most frequently asked question: Are you afraid?

Her answer: No.

She's wary, but not afraid.

"There's a lot of women who would like to do it, but who don't dare do it," Aura said. "They're intimidated of being in a car with strangers and of going places they've never been. But if women could just get past that …" her voice trails off.

Out of Aura's two hundred fellow drivers at Northside, seven are female, and most of them are wives of other drivers. Their husbands encourage them to take on the job for the cash and the flexibility.

That's how Aura came to the job.

She was working at McDonalds, and after her shift she would take a car to meet up with John, her partner and the father of her children. He worked as a dispatcher at Northside, and she would hang out with him at work. One night when it was really busy, there was a call in but no driver available.

"Do you want to take this guy?" John asked her.

"Of course, I'll take him!" said Aura, excited by the adventure.

She enjoyed it and decided to take a few more calls. Shortly thereafter, she got her TLC hack license.

"I saw how easy it was to drive people and make money," she said. "It wasn't hard work. It was relaxed."

She works odd hours, sometimes from 8 a.m. to 8 p.m. on Monday through Wednesday, sometimes she'll work Thursday, Friday and Saturday from 7 p.m. to 5 or 6 a.m. Sometimes she'll work, then pick the kids up from school, hang out with them over dinner, take them to karate, and go back to work. She stops when she feels tired, although sometimes she'll recharge by napping in the back of the car.

After watching her daughter do it, Aura's mother has since become a driver.

"All she needed was to see the money," Aura said.

Now, Aura is trying to convince her sister-in-law, who has a one-year-old at home, to drive.

General consensus says that driving for a car service is more dangerous than driving yellow cabs, as car service drivers operate in neighborhoods that taxis avoid. But Aura sees herself as safer than yellow cab drivers. True, Williamsburg and Greenpoint, Northside's

THE FAIRER SEX

~

Although Hillary Clinton nearly made it to the Oval Office, the glass ceiling in the cabbie world could use a few more cracks. Only about 1 percent of New York's 404,000-odd licensed cabbies are women. It's not that no one hires female cabbies—rather, it seems women aren't keen on sitting in a confined space with strangers while driving to unknown locations.

This tradition has held since women started driving cabs in New York, around the time they gained the right to vote. Only a few women braved the streets as cabbies during the Roaring Twenties, according to Graham Russell Gao Hodges, historian and author of *Taxi! A Social History of the New York City Cabdriver.* Their numbers remained miniscule until World War II, when thousands of men left for Europe or the Pacific and gals in sensible skirts took their place behind the wheel.

While a smattering of women continued to drive taxis over the next few decades, most stayed home with the kids and the dirty dishes. Women's Lib brought women into the workplace during the 1970s, but close on its heels was the deadly, gang-riddled 1980s—a scene that kept New York's fairer sex out of the driver's seat and further from harm's way.

home base neighborhoods, are hardly Brooklyn's most dangerous, unless hipsters leaving dodgeball games are viewed as a threat. She never picks up people who don't call ahead, and those who do call leave a phone number and address with Aura's dispatcher, making them traceable.

Aura also protects herself by refusing calls where potential passengers need lifts from rowdier bars.

She feels safe knowing other drivers have her back.

"We watch out for each other," she says. "Sometimes, customers give us a hard time by not paying or trying to fight with the driver or trying to rob the driver. But if [a driver] calls, gives the address and says they have a problem, everybody shoots over there to help. Usually we call the cops at the same time, but generally our cars get there first."

If the drivers arrive on the scene and there's a fight, they're ready. Aura has a small stick in her car and has taken a couple months of Tai Kwon Do.

"I'm not afraid to hit people," she says firmly.

She also has something else in her car to help her out of tough situations.

"I'm not going to tell you what it is, because it's got to be a surprise, but it's legal."

Aura's never had problems. She has a camera in the car, and passengers know it. Additionally, Northside's headquarters have cameras inside their offices and pointed towards the sidewalk.

Sure, she's had smaller issues. People bolting from the car without paying, for example. But if people start talking smack, or if sober people start making sexual comments that cross the line from funny to crude, she'll pull over and kick them out. The money's just not worth it.

"Don't mess with a driver late at night," she lectures. "We're working hard late at night to get you home safe. The least you can do is respect the driver."

Aura can usually tell if she's going to have a problem with someone as soon as they get into her car. Sometimes it's a vibe; sometimes, it's the way they talk.

"If they say, 'go to Graham and Grand,' and you get there, and they try to change the address, say, 'No!' You stop right there, because that's a problem."

Thieves use the address-changing tactic to lure drivers to shady neighborhoods or desolate corners and rob them.

"You have to remain in control," she says. "I'm the boss, I'm in control, I'm in charge. I'm driving you safe from A to B, and that's it. If it has to get physical, it has to get physical. You don't want it to get there, but God forbid, if somebody touch me, they're going to get hurt, you know what I'm saying? That's how it is. I can be really nice, educated and soft, but if you cross the line, you're gonna pay for that."

She refuses to pick up people who try and hail her from the street. First off, it's not legal—only yellow cabs are allowed to pick up street hails. Second, it's not safe—the dispatcher doesn't have a phone number or address to go with the passenger, and they may not be caught on camera.

One driver in her garage did pick up some random guy off the street near Kellogg's diner. He drove the man to the Bronx, where the guy robbed him at gunpoint, then took the car.

"He was lucky," Aura said. "He got the car back."

While she takes a hard line against passengers changing addresses, she does put up with a lot. She ignores drunks who talk trash because they're drunk, and their senses aren't right. She generally ignores guys who hit on her. However, once a British guy with a great sense of humor refused to get out of the car unless she kissed him. She relented a bit because he was cute and entertaining, and he settled for a kiss on the cheek. Another man offered to pay her for her time if she went into a club with him. She refused, in part because the guy was drunk, but also because she likes to wear make-up and look sexy when she dances, not wear work clothes.

Driving became more fun for Aura after her mother told her to eavesdrop on her customer's conversations. She listens mostly, but if she feels she has something positive to add, she'll give advice.

Her favorite combination of customers is having three women in the car.

"They will talk and talk about things that you won't imagine," she said, adding that it's mostly about boys, sex, and that day's events.

"It's really fun."

She also likes having three gay guys in the back of her cab for the exact same reasons—deep conversations about boys and sex.

"The gay guys in this area are so cute! And they smell good. They are so clean!"

Almost all her passengers treat her well, in part because she's a woman, she believes.

"Generally, when people see a female driver, they show a lot of respect," she says. "They see you and know that for you to be there, you have to be a strong person."

CURRIES LIKE MOM USED TO MAKE

~

The smell of cumin and coriander wafting down the street helps mark the easy-to-miss entrance of Punjabi Grocery & Deli, an East Village eatery favored by cabbies. Its front door sits below eye level, down a handful of crumbling stone steps, beside a nondescript garbage can. The unadorned entryway looks suspiciously like it someone's unlocked home, or maybe like an older bodega that has survived the area's gentrification. Additionally, the tree-lined median separating Houston Street and First Avenue nearly hides the entrance from Houston's foot traffic, although astute observers would notice a row of yellow cabs parked outside.

Like numerous other Indian and Pakistani joints around Manhattan, Punjabi opened to serve cabbies, who wanted food like their moms or wives made, but quickly and cheaply. Part fast-food place and part traditional restaurant, Punjabi's specifically intended clientele was Sikh drivers, many of whom came from India's Punjab region and grew up on vegetarian curries and thick dahls. But over the past few years, the inexpensive and tasty fare brought in a loyal following from the neighborhood. Today, band guys toting guitars and Latinos wearing Ecuadorian soccer jerseys eat standing next to the turban-clad Sikhs.

Once inside, the long narrow joint quickly overloads the senses— it has barely enough room to stand and eat. Behind the food display stretches a floor-to-ceiling explosion of colorful Bollywood DVDs, VHS tapes, and CDs of Indian music. Space beneath the counter is devoted to cases of bottled water and juice, while above the counter is imported packaged cookies, cough drops, gum and pre-paid phone cards. Patrons hang homemade signs, some in English, some not. One such sign advertises high-quality foam for taxi driver seats. Beside it is a laminated article about General Joginder Jaswant Singh, the first Sikh to lead India's army.

The customers line up cafeteria-style for the fragrant Indian food, heaped onto Styrofoam plates or into small Styrofoam bowls. Each order begins with white rice, cooked into a fluffy pile with no two grains sticking together. Patrons choose which steaming dishes are spooned on top; maybe zesty, puréed spinach, or okra simmered in a tomato-based curry, complimented by a thick lentil dahl or curried chickpeas. Then yogurt is drizzled over the meal and chopped red or white onions are tossed on top. All for less than five dollars.

"We are cheap and we are the best," said Billu Singh, twenty-seven, who runs the show. Singh, who came to the United States four years ago from India's Punjab region, has a vivacious personality, his smile wide as a game show hosts'. Singh's uncle opened the joint for the cab community more than ten years ago. His business has done so well, and New York's Indian community has grown so rapidly, that five years ago he opened a family restaurant in Jamaica Queens.

Three Indian women cook the food from scratch, delivering it to the restaurant twice a day. "They don't cook with butter," said Singh. "We want to keep our men healthy."

The vegetable selections change from day to day and season to season. In the fall they serve squash cooked with cumin and ginger, and sometimes they serve curried green peppers instead of okra. But every day they offer the drivers' favorites: the creamy spinach, the curried chickpeas, and the rich lentil dahl, which is also Singh's preferred dish. On the long nearby counter, clear plastic measuring cups hold small pieces of curried mango, hot and tart in an involuntary pucker kind of way.

For those needing to wash down the spicy fare, towards the back of the restaurant an orange, beat-up igloo water cooler sits on a stand, small disposable cups to one side. The water is free for anyone who needs it.

The trickiest part of Punjabi is finding space to comfortably chow down. The tight walkway between the food display on the right and the narrow counter on the left is close enough that no more than two people can comfortably stand back-to-back. Most diners amicably take their food to the far end of the counter, where they stand and eat. The place wasn't designed for a sit-down meal; it's made for cab drivers who only take fifteen-minute breaks, because any time not working equals less money they send to their families in India.

Although Singh knows many of his customers—he addresses many cabbies by name and calls out "My man!" to other regulars—he claims to know zero cabbie gossip. Most of the drivers only stop in

His Heart is in His Stomach

~

New York hosts a number of hole-in-the-wall eateries that serve up flaky samosas, thick dahls, fragrant garlic nan, curried rice pilaf, tender lamb, and moist tandoori chicken. Catering to their cabbies, these restaurants are tasty, speedy, cheap and vegetarian friendly.

Punjabi Grocery & Deli: 114 East 1st St., between 1rst Ave. and Avenue A; 212-533-9048. Tasty and cheap, with Bollywood DVDs to boot!

Haandi: 113 Lexington Ave. between 27nd St. and 28rd St.; 212-685-5200. Just follow the line of yellow cabs to Haandi's door.

Pakistan Tea House: 176 Church St. between Duane St. and Reade St.; 212-240-9800. Lower Manhattan's favorite stopping spot: Some of their meals are as expensive as—gasp!— eight dollars. But don't worry, most cost less than five dollars.

Lahore: 132 Crosby St., between Houston St. and Jersey St.; 212-965-1777. Named after the city in the Punjab province, and handily (for cabbies) located across the street from one of Houston Street's gas stations.

Curry in a Hurry: 119 Lexington at 28th St.; 212-683-0900. Conveniently located in a neighborhood called "Curry Hill," the food tastes as good as the neighborhood smells.

Dil-e Punjab: 170 Ninth Ave., near 20th St.; 212-647-9428. The best place to hide from the über-chic Meatpacking hordes and get your eat on, too.

for ten or fifteen minutes; rarely do they stick around for idle chit chat. "They don't have time," he said. "Gas is costly. They need more money."

Singh and his uncle understand the cab drivers needs. They serve cheap, healthy and familiar food and sell them Indian music for their taxis. They offer free water. And importantly, they always let drivers use their restroom, even if they don't order a cup of chai this time around. "I know they will be back later," Singh said. He understands how difficult it is to find a restroom or parking in Manhattan.

REVOLUTIONARY POLITICS BEHIND THE WHEEL

~

A ngry at Republican plans to hold their 2004 National Convention in his hometown of New York, John McDonagh, a founder of Cabbies Against Bush, or CAB, sprang into action.

By the time the Republicans came to town, John was ready. His plan? To hand out coupons for free yellow cab rides to Kennedy or Newark airports for "any Republican delegate, right-wing talk show host, or any other chicken hawk who, during the Republican Convention, feels the patriotic urge go to Iraq and do battle."

Fliers went up urging cabbies to keep their lights on during the day, shining a light on Bush's war policies. The fliers encouraged passengers to ask their cabbies to turn on the lights.

He even extended his offer of a free cab ride to Fox News pundit Bill O'Reilly—but only if O'Reilly had a one-way ticket to Baghdad.

John wrote in a press release explaining his campaign: "As our War President said, it is better to fight them there than here. Yellow cab drivers will sleep better knowing that Wild Bill O'Reilly is fighting to keep us free."

He even went so far as to hold a press conference outside Fox News' headquarters. After giving his speech, John stalked into the building and handed over a coupon specifically for O'Reilly. His bold move landed him on Fox television for one minute and fifty-two seconds. After that, he was cut off.

No Republican delegates took him up on the offer. Not that John cared.

"See, that was a creative way of using my cab," said John, a Queens native. "It's not about getting stuck in the mundane and getting a nine-millimeter stuck to your head in the South Bronx. I use my cab to push my politics."

The fair-skinned son of Irish immigrants, he considers the Irish Republican Movement his main political passion. When John talks about politics—which is basically all the time—his intensity boils over, and you can almost see his muscles wind like springs. His vehemence and quick wit leads you to believe that, despite being middle aged, John could take just about anybody in a fight, verbal or physical.

John's political beliefs are, as he says, "European socialist." Most Americans would call him a Marxist.

Like many true "European socialists," John would sacrifice his own income for his beliefs. John lambasted Mayor Michael Bloomberg's proposal to battle Manhattan's traffic congestion by charging drivers eight dollars to enter Manhattan below Eighty-sixth Street during weekday working hours. He sees it as an unfair tax on the outer borough working class. He doesn't care that the plans' implementation would mean more customers and fewer crowded streets for taxi drivers.

As someone who dependably roots for the underdog, it's hardly surprising that he's a Mets fan.

John's activism and his cabbie career came about after he voluntarily enlisted in the army at the end of the Vietnam War. He never made it further than Germany. By the time his tour ended, the war had turned him against government. Afterwards, he hitchhiked around the world for a year, hitting Australia, New Zealand, Indonesia, Singapore and Thailand before going through Europe and returning to New York, where he sought out a union job. His sister was a cop and his brothers were in the elevator union, so John found a job as a cab driver.

The job's flexibility gave him time to dedicate to the Irish Republican movement and the Irish Republican Army, a popular cause in his Irish-American neighborhood.

He took time off and flew to Ireland during the 1981 Irish hunger strike, where he watched ten Irish Republican prisoners starve themselves to death. He raised money in the United States for Sinn Fein's political prisoners. He hasn't driven on Saturdays for twenty years. Instead, he produced and hosted an Irish news radio show, Radio Free Eireann, broadcasted Saturday afternoons over New York's left-wing WBAI 99.5 FM. (Sometimes, he used his slot to broadcast taxi-related shows). The station's offices are ironically located on Wall Street.

He met all types as editor of the U.S.-based newspaper *Irish People*. Once, the Feds burst through the doors to the paper's offices. Everyone at the paper yelled out, then froze. John asked the officers for their warrant. They laughed. They wanted the guy working the paper's phones—Hugh Feeney, an Irishman previously convicted of setting off two bombs in London, killing one and injuring nearly two hundred.

One of John's less fortunate colleagues at the paper, top Sinn Fein operative Denis Donaldson, was exposed as a long-time British spy in

TLC, NOT TENDER LOVING CARE

~

Any conversation with cab drivers will inadvertently be peppered with the acronym TLC—standing for the New York City Taxi and Limousine Commission. The agency, formed in 1971 to regulate the city's transportation, is responsible for running New York City's drivers-for-hire. Consequently, drivers view the TLC as a group of malevolent Gods on high. The TLC, after all, gives out tickets, charges fines, and has the ability to suspend their licenses. While we may associate the letters TLC with tender loving care, cabbies use a completely different set of words—the phrase "tells lies constantly" has been heard. The TLC regulates more than 50,000 vehicles and 100,000 drivers, including yellow cabs, limos and car services.

Thanks to the TLC's specifics, drivers have a dress code: no bathing trunks, no underwear worn outside the clothes and no wife beaters, thank you very much. Additionally, drivers are forbidden to deliver property unaccompanied by its owner—unless the property is blood or human organs (we're seriously hoping a hospital is the destination here). And if you're looking to buy a knock-off DVD, street corners and subway stations remain the best places to do so, as the TLC forbids drivers to sell goods or services from their cabs.

2002. He was hunted down at his remote hiding place and shot in the head shortly thereafter. The real IRA claimed responsibility.

John's Irish-American involvement even scored him a role as an extra in Martin Scorsese's film, *The Departed*.

John stresses his minimal role in the Irish movement. He wasn't a leader. He was only one of the spokes in the wheel. All the Irish-Americans he grew up with were involved. He just did his bit, that's all. And he's not spending five-to-seven years in the slammer, unlike some poor guys, he says.

The favorite bit he did for the movement occurred in the early 1980s. The idea popped into his head while he was stopped at a red light in seedy Times Square during the holiday season. While he normally watched traffic while driving, for some reason, this day he looked up. Unlike the festival of flashing lights and advertisements there today, back then Times Square had only one television-like sign, flashing mundane messages like "happy birthday!"

John's brain went into high gear. He called an artist friend and asked him to design a pro-IRA ad. He traveled from Irish pub to Irish pub and begged two thousand bucks off the beer-guzzling clientele. Then John put on a suit and visited the sign's owner, purchasing the use of the sign. The owner guaranteed him any advertisement he chose would flash across Times Square one minute out of every ten.

The day the ad aired, John sat drinking a beer in the Times Square pub, the Blarney Stone.

"Yes!" he yelled when the ad flash across the screen. It read: "Merry Christmas to all the Irish Prisoners of War in America, Ireland and England. Ireland Gaelic and Free." The graphic was a picture of Ireland with the boarder between north and south blowing up. John signed it UTP, which stood for Up the Provos, proclaiming support for the provisional wing of the IRA.

As the IRA had almost blown up Prime Minister Margaret Thatcher in her hotel room shortly before John's ad ran, journalists from around the world leapt on the story. Headlines shouted that the IRA hijacked Times Square.

"See, that was another creative way of using my cab," John says. "I was driving, then I looked up."

Not having a boss gave John the flexibility to travel to Nicaragua and monitor elections for the United Nations, all while the Reagan-funded Contras fought the Sandinistas. John also used the time to deliver tapes to IRA guys on the lam—he found them hanging out at a pub with members of the Palestine Liberation Organization and militants from the African National Congress, South Africa's anti-apartheid party.

Not surprisingly, John despised the U.S.-funded Contras.

"It wasn't a fair election. I saw that the pharmacies didn't have any drugs. I talked to someone saying that if they elected the [anti-American] opposition, the embargo would keep up, and they'd still have no medicine."

John took action and began a radio broadcast from a Salvadorian bar in Nicaragua's capital, Managua.

"We denounced the American government," he said. "I saw how we controlled that election. All this bullshit about free elections? Whatever."

John would challenge anyone who called him anti-American.

"I just want to make this country a better place."

Despite his socialist leanings, John works America's capitalist system like an expert. He enjoys driving and speaking with many of his passengers, but first and foremost, he's there to make money.

For example, when he traverses the wealthy Upper East Side late in the morning, he avoids picking up people with wheelchairs or walkers.

"You get stuck in this medical vortex of the Upper East Side, where they're trying to flag you down, you have to get out and break your back putting their walker in the trunk. Then you get to the hospital—and *voila*—who's coming out of the doctor's office but somebody else in a fricking wheelchair, and they want to come back to the Upper East Side because they're too cheap to take an ambulance."

He says he's not unsympathetic to their plight, but he is pragmatic.

Why should he pay because America's health care system doesn't take care of its people?

If tourists pay him for an hour-long tour, John will happily cart them around—but he chooses his routes carefully. He prefers to cruise down Manhattan's west side on the FDR Drive for two reasons. First, it keeps his meter ticking, and he gets a better rate. Second, the route takes him past a slew of sites, including the Williamsburg, Manhattan and Brooklyn Bridges.

He doesn't much enjoy tourists who seem like the type to not agree with his politics. He can generally spot them, with one sign being a southern accent. Every once in a while, a Republican-looking tourist will try and engage John by asking his opinion of George W. Bush. John has a pat answer.

"He should be tried as a war criminal and then executed," he says, and then he turns the radio up.

CHAPTER 6

HOOKING UP

Sex, Love, and the Yellow Cab

An effortless way to research this book involved walking into a party, spreading the word that I needed true taxi stories, and waiting for people to approach me with their tales. A few drinks in, and people's stories morphed from 'this cool cabbie I met' to cab sex. And judging by the excited edge their voices took on, most people I spoke with enjoyed sharing their fervid escapades in the back of a cab. The narratives ranged from innocent late-night kisses to a fighting-for-legroom *ménage à trois*. Many men and women fondly referred to taxicab fellatio as a special, but not unexpected, treat, like receiving flowers on Valentine's Day or spending a weekend at the beach.

Before anecdotally learning of the normalcy of sex in cabs, I already suspected New Yorkers had a special relationship with exhibitionism. I never lived anywhere else where so many people shared details of trysts in dive bar bathrooms, on elevators and in Central Park's crowded Sheep Meadow on a Saturday afternoon. But why the proclivity for such "outdoor activities?"

There are slews of speculative reasons.

First off, much of New York is young, liberal and decently affluent.

On top of that, the city itself nurtures a culture of permissiveness and encourages risk. In the spirit of "why not have fun?" it seems only natural.

Additionally, we all live on top of each other here. Nothing is private. I know what the couple upstairs from my apartment fights about, and hear them make up afterwards. If you forget to pull down your blinds at night, you'll have a dozen neighbors peering into your bedroom. With so much of your life already open to strangers, having sex against a building in a dark alley may not seem like such a big deal.

Also, there doesn't seem to be much repercussion for being caught *il flagrante*. Apparently thrice-married Giuliani's crackdown on "quality of life" crimes bypassed public indecency. I've only heard of one couple being prosecuted for lewdness, and these particular Virginians were caught in a vestibule of the revered St. Patrick's Cathedral.

Plus cabs hold a special allure for New Yorkers. Maybe it's the ease of settling into the backseat. Maybe it's the fact that tipsy couples are on their way home to have sex and think of the ride as foreplay. And, of course, there's the extra jolt of knowing someone—the driver—could be watching.

Not that the cabbies themselves aren't complicit. I wasn't comfortable asking every driver I spoke with about sex. (My polite Midwestern roots resulted in my shying away from even mentioning the word to certain drivers). But those I did ask admitted to frequently fielding—and sometimes accepting—late night propositions from both men and women. Front seat, back seat, the inside of their passenger's apartment—cabbies have seen it all. They see even more through the rearview mirror. While some admit annoyance when people use their cab as a bedroom, others don't mind playing the role of voyeur.

Anyway, the idea of sex in cabs has been around for ages, probably since cabs were invented. Former cab driver and social historian Graham Russell Gao Hodges has a collection of taxi postcards from the mid-twentieth century. On one postcard, the cabbie asks his fare, getting hot and heavy with a busty lady in the backseat, "How far would you like to go, sir?"

In this chapter, the answer is "All the way."

LUCK OF THE DRAW

~

Susan Blitz * and her new Australian boyfriend, Nathan, grabbed a cab to take them to Nathan's Midtown hotel. They normally stayed at her Brooklyn apartment when he visited from London. This time, though, he was on a business trip and his company put him up.

Once in the cab, they began kissing, which progressed to light petting. Susan straddled Nathan's lap to get a better angle on the situation.

The two had met through a mutual friend six months earlier at the U.S. Open. Nathan was hard to miss, especially when seated near members of Long Island's country clubs. Not only did he wear a green and yellow cape—Australia's colors—but he carried around a plastic alligator, and, together with his friends, drunkenly yelled "Aussie, Aussie, Aussie . . . Oi, Oi, Oi!" whenever an Australian took the court. Nathan adored Susan's impulsivity, love of dogs, intelligence, and willingness to try anything at once. Susan, a feisty woman who inherited her dark hair and sharp features from Italian and Yugoslavian grandparents, appreciated his height—he stood well over six feet—and fell for his sense of humor.

After riding in the taxi for about a minute, the cab came to a screeching halt. At first Susan and Nathan thought there was an accident. They stopped briefly, but as they saw no shattered glass and heard no one yelling, they got back to business.

"You filthy animals!" the cab driver shouted. "You are a disgrace!"

Susan figured he was yelling at someone on the street. Maybe a drunken pedestrian had lunged off the curb and in front of the cab, making their driver slam on the brakes.

"You filthy animals! You get out now!" he screamed.

Susan turned around. She realized the driver was talking to them.

"Get out! Filthy animals!" he repeated.

She and Nathan hastily exited the cab, trying not to giggle. Before they could pay him, he sped off.

Standing near the curb, he couple broke into laughter. Susan nearly bent over double.

"Oh my God, I'm a whore!"

"Well, at least half the ride was free," Nathan joked.

While she found the situation incredibly funny—not least because she'd had sex in cabs twice before without repercussion—she also suffered a brief crisis of conscience.

"I can't believe it," she said wiping away her tears. "He's deeply religious and I've just offended him with my brutish American ways!"

Nathan howled, and she started laughing again.

They hailed another cab.

They got in the backseat, still giggling, and Nathan kissed her.

"No, no! Get off me!" she shrieked, fending him off. "We've got to actually get to the hotel. We can't get kicked out again!"

They both laughed, he sat back, and Susan leaned up to the partition.

"Excuse me," she said to the driver, who, like the previous one, looked like a middle-aged Middle Eastern man. "Do people ever make out or have sex in your cab?"

"Yes, all the time," he said good-naturedly. "In fact, some people get into my cab just to have sex."

"Really?" she said. "Because we just got kicked out of our last cab for making out. And we were hardly even doing anything!"

The driver chuckled. "Oh, he just needs to get laid."

Susan and Nathan laughed.

"You can make out in my cab any time," he said. "I don't care. Just don't leave a mess."

BROOKLYN BRIDGE BANG

~

Tyler Russo* left a Lower East Side party with his girlfriend, Tammy. As he went to hail a cab, Tammy looked at him.

"I want to do something I've never done before," she said in a saucy voice.

She was a little drunk. Tyler knew what her tone meant.

He braced himself.

"We're going to fuck in a cab going over the Brooklyn Bridge," she said.

His eyebrows rose.

"Why don't we see what happens," he said in a slightly wavering voice that he attempted to disguise with a macho expression.

He needed to hedge for time.

He felt a jolt of excitement at the opportunity to do something together that she had never done before. Especially as it seemed she had done everything with her ex.

He didn't want to have sex on the bridge, but he didn't want to lose Tammy's attention either.

He hoped no cab would come. He needed time to think.

He leaned in and kissed Tammy. He could smell sexuality in her long brown hair. She had a slow, sensual way of moving that highlighted curves more than her provocative clothes ever could. Tyler dug the fact that other men wanted his girlfriend, but he wished Tammy didn't feed so greedily on their attention.

A cab came. Tyler took a good look at the driver as he pulled up. He appeared to be in his mid-thirties, and had short hair and a beard. He could have been Indian, or maybe Pakistani.

"We're going to Brooklyn Heights, just across the Brooklyn Bridge," Tyler told the driver.

Once in the cab, he reached over to Tammy and kissed her, running his fingers up her thigh. They always did this on the way home—he saw it as a bit of exhibitionistic fun, but with no one able to see.

Tammy wanted more. She pounced on him like a tiger, her hands all over his body. He pretended to go with it, but maneuvered her off his lap.

They had done a lot over the past six months. She pushed him, and he responded. He had never been so sexually adventurous in his life. On a cross-country road trip, they screwed behind every highway truck stop they could find. They did it on the edge of Central Park's Sheep Meadow in broad daylight. Tammy was on top, an accurate metaphor for their relationship. He wished she were as crazy about him as he was about her.

Tammy went for Tyler's pants. His long legs and height worked against him in the cramped backseat, while Tammy darted around like a nymph. But he managed to distract her again with kisses as the cab cruised through side streets, parting groups of pedestrians.

He was a more than willing participant, but it didn't come naturally to him. He had a fear of consequences that Tammy didn't share. He came from a line of Irish drunks who could wind up on the wrong side of the law any given weekend. He knew no officer would charge Tammy with indecency.

Tyler knew he couldn't control Tammy much longer. He tried pinning her arms behind her back while he kissed her, but she outmaneuvered him and unzipped his pants.

"Oh yeah!" she said.

Tyler whipped his head around, paranoid that every nearby driver and person with binoculars in the neighboring buildings could see him. He was completely exposed as the cab slowly moved through side streets and stopped for a red light. Oh, God, anyone could watch! Cars passed them going the other direction. What if he got collared on a pervert rap?

When they reached the service ramp to the bridge, Tammy tried yanking his pants to his knees. Tyler surrendered and helped her, figuring compliance was the fastest way out of this mess. Her aggressive move made him hot, but he cringed at the feel of his bare ass on the dirty vinyl seat.

Wasting no time, Tammy pushed her skirt up to her waist like a fruit rollup and slung one leg over his lap, facing him. She steadied herself with her hands on his shoulders.

His sweaty ass stuck to the backseat.

Tammy moved quickly, knowing her apartment was right on the other side of the bridge. Tyler was turned on, but he focused on containing the situation.

"You think you should tone it down a little bit?" he asked, putting his hands on her hips to slow her.

"Don't worry about it," she said as she ran a hand through his dark hair.

Sitting in the middle of the backseat, Tyler looked through the partition's window and saw the driver watching them through his rearview mirror. They made eye contact. Tyler felt decidedly uncomfortable.

"Oh yes, yes," Tammy moaned.

"The driver's watching us," Tyler whispered, running one hand over Tammy's chest.

"Don't worry about it," she said, her face flushed.

He caught the driver's eye in the mirror again. Didn't this guy ever look at the road?

Tyler tried to pull Tammy's skirt down so the driver couldn't see her white butt. It didn't work.

Tyler moved his hands to her waist and unfastened the last few buttons on her shirt. He left her top on to make their act less obvious, although he knew she wanted him to tear it off.

He met the driver's eyes in the mirror for a third time. This round, Tyler held his gaze. If the driver focused on him, he couldn't look at what they were doing. He didn't enjoy the driver watching, although Tammy wanted just that. There was something disturbingly erotic about his presence. The driver seemed to be participating, as if they were having a threesome.

At this point, Tammy threw off all pretense of having a polite tryst and started moving harder and faster. If the taxi's roof hadn't been there, she would have thrown her head back.

"This is fucking great," she said.

"You maybe want to be less obvious?" Tyler whispered.

He put his hands on her hips, trying to steady her and make her motions less flamboyant.

"The driver is watching us."

"Don't worry," she said.

A car drove by. A passenger looked in the cab and hooted gleefully. Immediately, three heads hung out of the car's unrolled windows, cheering them on. With his pants at his knees and Tammy's skirt around her waist, Tyler knew anyone passing in an SUV could see every detail.

Then Tyler almost flipped. The cabbie was staring at them again, but this time not through the mirror. His hand was on the wheel, but he had managed to turn his neck around and stick his head through the partition window. He was not facing the road. The car careened through space, and Tyler willed it to stay in the lane. All his energy had to go towards keeping them on the bridge.

The driver's expression was serious as his eyes fixed on Tammy's ass. His face was only one foot away from her back.

Tyler could not believe it. He was the only one facing the road. What the hell was the cabbie doing?

Tyler reached out and pushed his hand against the cabbie's face, his long fingers spread out and sinking into the driver's skin. The driver's expression was furious: eyes wide, lips pulled back and teeth bared. He nearly growled. Tammy, oblivious, pumped away. Tyler could feel the scratchiness of the driver's beard against his hand, the guy's doughy nose squishing between his fingers.

It was a brutally animalistic moment. As Tyler pushed harder, a feeling of power rushed through him. It wasn't the usual power that came with sex. At that moment, he became the man his girlfriend wanted, the man who feared nothing. He became aware of every inch of his height and every muscle in his body. He grew older, manlier and tougher. He was a force.

The driver turned back to the road. Tyler saw the approaching red light at the end of the bridge. He would have to give directions home, as Tammy wouldn't care if they ended up in Sheepshead Bay. The end in sight, Tyler increased the pace. He wanted to finish before they reached her apartment.

"This is fucking awesome," she said, "Yes, yes!"

The driver stopped at the light. "Make a right here," said Tyler, intent on his goal.

They stopped at the light. A car pulled up beside them and the passengers rubber-necked to watch them, catcalling. Tyler's heart beat like a jackhammer. The feeling of the driver's beard on his hand remained fresh in Tyler's mind. He felt like they sat at the light for forty-five minutes. Why wouldn't it change?

Tammy shuddered as the light turned green. Tyler took control and more or less threw her off his lap. He pulled her skirt down and pulled his own pants up as he directed the driver to a corner near Tammy's place—he didn't want the cabbie knowing where she lived.

The driver stopped and an awkward silence engulfed them. Tyler looked at the meter, handed the guy a twenty and said, "I'll take six dollars back." They avoided eye contact, but Tyler saw in the mirror that the man wasn't smiling. Without turning around, the driver handed six dollars though the partition window.

They got out. Tyler felt a terrifically discomforting familiarity with the driver. He and Tammy walked to her apartment. Tyler hoped to never see the driver again in his life.

SOMEONE WHO CARES

~

Chloe Birnbäumer* and her boyfriend Andrea had an electric connection. She met him at the East Village bar beloved by international jet-setters, NuBlu. Chloe approached Andrea's friend, mistaking him for a drummer she hoped to recruit for her jazz band. Andrea, then a stranger, strode up to them, looked into Chloe's eyes and said, "I'm from Venice, let me show you how we greet people in my country." He kissed her full on.

Chloe's heart melted faster than the ice cubes in her pricey cranberry vodka cocktail.

Andrea had charisma, and his passion for Chloe was explosive. On their third date, Andrea's jealous female roommate interrupted a kiss between him and Chloe, plied them apart and started screaming at Andrea in Italian. Chloe ran out of the bar and Andrea chased her all over the West Village, screaming her name in his thick accent, yelling, "You must trust me, you must trust me!"

Chloe always felt that the men who chased her loved her most, a fact that helped explain her history of being stalked.

She fell for Andrea every time he carried her out of the apartment, her arms twisted around his neck. Not unimportantly, their sessions between the sheets were vivid, sweaty and steaming hot.

She loved him and wanted to trust him completely, but somehow couldn't. There were always other women around, women who gave Chloe dirty looks, and Chloe couldn't discern their status. Once, a female friend of Andrea's visited from Italy and stayed in his apartment. He refused to see Chloe during the whole week of her visit. She was crushed, screamed at him and called him a cheater, but he won her back with soft words and kisses.

After making love, he would tell her that he loved her, that he wanted to marry her and have babies.

"If we're going to have a family, let's do it!" he'd say.

The next day he would change his mind, telling Chloe he didn't know if he wanted to settle down.

But Chloe couldn't pull herself away. When their relationship worked, it was incredible. He was like crack. True, he did terrible things. But he loved his mother so much and spoke of her with such reverence that Chloe couldn't believe he was really this bad.

She kept waiting. Tall and slender, with straight sleek hair, Chloe could have easily found someone else. Men always noticed her in a bar. She made tons of money working in technology for an investment bank, and men adored her alter-ego as a sultry jazz singer, especially when she wore wigs onstage.

Eight months in to their relationship, Andrea broke up with Chloe in the middle of the street on her birthday, yelling "No! I don't want to see you!" while Chloe cried wildly and screamed.

But Andrea couldn't keep away. One month later, they met at a Cuban restaurant. He sat next to her and tried to pull her closer. He told her that he loved her. He said that in one year, they would get married and have a baby. A few days later, he told her he didn't want to be in a relationship. It was the same story. Chloe tried to keep her distance, physically and emotionally, and they danced around each other for a few months. She couldn't get him out of her mind. She knew he was poison, but she needed him.

They got back together.

They stayed happy for two months before they began arguing, once again, about marriage and children. Chloe wanted both, and soon. Andrea changed his mind. He wanted none of it. The screaming matches became unbearable. They split up.

The next month ambiguity reigned. One minute they had compassionate conversations, the next they hurled insults at each other, always making up in bed. The back-and-forth was endless. Then one night he called her up at 2 a.m. after being out at a bar.

"I feel different," he said. "I don't want to see you anymore. I feel different."

Chloe heard in his voice that something had changed. She started to cry, her mind spinning.

"If we're going to break up, let's not do it over the phone," she said. "I have a birthday gift for you. I'll come over to your apartment, we can talk, and I'll give you your gift."

"Come on over," he said. "I'll be waiting for you."

She hung up the phone, ran out of her apartment, hopped in a cab and arrived at the doorstep of his Lower East Side apartment within five minutes. She rang his bell. He didn't answer. She rang the bell for the next thirty minutes and called his cell phone repeatedly. He still didn't answer.

It was the final humiliation. Not only did he refuse to marry her, but he didn't even have the decency to be home when they were ending their relationship. She started crying inconsolably. She threw his birthday gift—a book on finding your calling—in a garbage can near his building and phoned him one last time.

"Your gift is in the garbage," she screamed into his voicemail. "I'm not going to let you hurt me again!"

She began stumbling towards her apartment on Fourteenth Street and Avenue A, about fourteen blocks away. She was so distraught and crying so hard that she couldn't walk properly. She staggered up the sidewalk. Within a few minutes a cab pulled to the curb. The cabbie unrolled his window.

"Ma'am, ma'am!" he called to her, leaning out the window. "Miss, miss! Get in the car. I'll take you where you need to go."

She managed to answer with a strangled, "No thank you."

"Are you sure?" he pleaded. "Come on, get in."

"No, I'm fine," she insisted, her voice sounding nasally through her tears. "I really want to walk."

"Okay," he said and sped off.

She continued down the street, weeping loudly and wiping her eyes. Three blocks later, a second cab stopped.

"Miss, are you okay?" he called to her. "Do you need a ride? Let me give you a ride home."

"No, no," she said through her tears. "Thanks, but I'd rather walk."

"Are you sure?" he said. "I can take you where you need to go."

"I know, thanks," she answered. "I'm fine."

The taxi drove on and Chloe, immersed in her misery stumbled on. Within a few more blocks later, a third cabbie stopped beside her.

"You want a ride?" he asked through the open window.

"No," Chloe answered.

"Can I please help you?" he pressed.

"No," she sniffed. "I'm okay."

In fact, she was feeling better. Andrea was a jerk, yet the world didn't seem so bad. She couldn't believe that she had walked only seven blocks and three cab drivers had stopped to help her. She must look terrible. But the driver's kindness and humanity impressed her. It cheered her up, if only a bit.

"At least somebody cares!" she thought.

MEDALLION STALLION

~

In the late 1980s, Michael Greenberg* picked up an attractive woman near gritty Tompkins Square Park on Avenue A.

"I'm going to Eighty-eighth and Riverside," she said, mentioning one of the posher drives in Manhattan.

Michael checked out her long legs and curves through the rearview mirror. She had a Halle Berry-esque pixie cut, which framed her heart-shaped face. Her dress clung to her body, accentuating her curves with simplicity and taste. Michael didn't often pick up well-dressed people in this seedy part of town—especially not by such a well-known crack park.

They started chit-chatting politely, but her conversation rapidly got raunchier when she started complaining about two guys who wanted her to do all sorts of things.

"What am I, Miss Pussy?" she said. "Miss Ass? I'm not going to do all that stuff!"

Michael knew the answer. She wasn't classy—she just looked it.

"You shouldn't do what you're not comfortable with doing," he said. "If you're not comfortable, it's a no go!"

"Right on," she said.

With a body like that, Michael gathered she worked as a high-priced hooker, hence her Riverside Drive destination.

She cocked her head.

"Listen, you ever have your dick sucked while you're driving?"

Michael paused before answering, trying to figure out if it was a question or an offer. He didn't want to offend her by assuming it was an offer, but he also didn't want to let this opportunity pass. He decided simple was better.

"No."

She launched herself over the seat and landed next to him.

"I was driving on the West Side Highway, and God bless her," he said. "She slapped that condom on and we were off to the races."

They arrived at her destination shortly after she was finished. The silence grew. The meter read seven dollars.

"You don't have to pay," Michael said awkwardly.

"Keep the change," she said, handing him a ten-dollar bill. "And can I have a receipt?"

DOCTOR LOVE

~

Zevesh Chandra*, who moved to the United States from India when he was seventeen, reads voraciously about psychology. The subject fascinates him, and he and his friends often sit around discussing it. Their favorite subjects: The passengers riding in the back of Zevesh's taxi.

"In this city, the biggest problem is the relationship problem," says Zevesh, an attractive man in his mid-thirties with a classic Roman profile, shaved head, and body fit for the cover of *Men's Health*. "People don't want to change until somebody else changes. But really, nobody wants to change because they are dreaming. But it's a dream that won't take you anywhere."

He believes he knows the root of New Yorker's problems with relationships and dreams: selfishness. People think only their feelings matter. People also become obsessed with meaningless material possessions.

Zevesh blames American parents who don't teach kids to share.

"You take a bite out of a kid's food, and see how they react," Zevesh says. "If they let you eat their food, good. Then, when they're eighteen or twenty, they learn to share their problems with other people. When you don't learn sharing as a kid, you don't know how to do it as an adult."

Many New Yorkers don't share their problems with those they love, Zevesh sees. Instead, they share with taxi drivers.

Cheating

One night, a couple fighting in the street hailed his cab. Before getting in, the man slammed his fist into Zevesh's windshield in frustration.

The woman cried as the man called her a bitch and a whore. The two fought about family—who told whose mother and sister what information. Zevesh watched them through the rearview mirror. She was a beautiful woman with long, straight black hair, East Asian eyes and a slender figure. Zevesh wanted to slap the man.

In the middle of their argument, the man had enough.

"Pull over," he said to Zevesh. "Pull over!"

Zevesh stopped and the man jumped out, slamming the door and leaving the woman alone in the cab.

The woman sniffed in the back seat.

"Are you okay?" Zevesh asked.

She nodded, then started talking.

She was married to the man who leapt out of the cab. They dated for six years before tying the knot two years ago. Tonight, they had gone to a dinner at an expensive restaurant with a famous chef. When the pair waited at the bar before being seated, the woman spilled her beer. Because of her mistake, her husband yelled at her in the middle of the bar, calling her names and embarrassing her. She had started crying. Then they left and got into Zevesh's cab.

The woman looked at Zevesh and regretted speaking ill of her husband.

"He works hard," she said, excusing him.

"Yes, but the way he acts in public, it doesn't make sense," Zevesh said. "How many times has he done this month? Is this the second time?"

"No, it's the third time," she said.

Zevesh came to his conclusion.

"He's definitely having an affair on the side."

"What?!" said the woman.

"Does he get mad about little things, and then leave you home alone?" Zevesh asked. "Then, does he come back in the morning and apologize?"

"Yes," she said softly.

"And that doesn't ring an alarm bell for you?"

"What do you mean?" she asked.

"He does this on purpose! He wants to spend the night out, so he has to make a big scene and get all pissed off so he can leave you alone.

That way, you think he's just mad at you, and you don't expect him back until morning."

Zevesh continued.

"In the morning when he comes back, is he a very happy man?" he asked.

"Yes, he brings me flowers and he kisses me," she said. "He says I love you."

"Oh, no, that's not good," Zevesh said. "Watch out!"

He pulled up to her building. The doorman watched the woman speak with Zevesh.

"Clean your eyes and don't tell anyone anything," Zevesh told her. "Keep it to yourself, but call your mother."

"I don't have a good relationship with my mother," she said.

For Zevesh, this explained everything.

"That's your biggest problem!" Zevesh told her. "Your mother is the best thing in your life."

"But we're different," she said.

"Listen, honey, never blame your parents for anything, because they did the best that they could do for us. Maybe they had many problems. It's not easy with kids."

"I want to go to the doctor," she listlessly said.

"Doctors won't do nothing," Zevesh chided. "He'll give you some pills. You'll go to sleep and wake up with the same problems. You need to talk to your husband."

She got out of the cab.

After a few years of watching people in his cab, Zevesh believed he learned to tell when people are cheating on each other. It's in the timing of a joke, the good-bye kiss, or the brief touch of a hand. Nothing is set, yet it always makes sense to him. He's seen guys leave girlfriends behind in his cab, only to have the woman call another guy the minute Zevesh pulls out into traffic.

He's seen people who stay in bad relationships because they are lonely. They don't care how badly their partner treats them, as long as they have someone.

Fool's Love

Yet another feuding pair got into his cab. He knew they were in a relationship even before he heard what they said. Only couples fight so fiercely.

"But you told me you love me!" the girl howled. "You e-mailed me that you love me! You said I was the best thing in your life! We've been together for three years. Why has this suddenly changed?"

"I'm just drunk," the guy said. "I don't know what I like and what I don't like."

Zevesh watched the woman stare at her boyfriend.

"You told me when we went to dinner that you were ready for a relationship, you were ready for everything, and now, only hours later, you're changing your mind?" she said, panic in her voice.

"I just think now isn't a good time to start something," he said.

"You've been with me for three years, you e-mail me and tell me you love me, that you care about me . . . what is this?" she cried.

The guy stayed silent for a minute.

"Maybe I'm drunk," he eventually said. "I don't know. I'm sorry if I've hurt your feelings."

Zevesh watched them in the mirror. He felt for the woman. He had been in love and dumped, too, but not like this. His girlfriend had loved him for many years. She dumped him and broke his heart after they moved from Texas to New York and she found someone else. Now he lived alone in his Queens apartment.

But whether or not this man knew it, he had played with his girlfriend's heart and brain for three years. He treated her like a toy that he could buy and then take back if he got bored.

This guy was afraid of getting his feelings hurt, Zevesh thought. He was so scared that he preferred to be single. Yes, he was in a relationship, but with someone he didn't love. It was as good as being single.

How selfish, Zevesh thought.

Superficiality

Average-looking people with average bodies and average faces have a better chance at happy marriages, Zevesh believes. At least no one uses them for their beauty.

Last year, Zevesh spoke with a pretty woman putting on make-up in his cab.

"Sweetie, you look like you're going on a date," he said.

"No," she laughed, "but I'm looking!"

"What are you looking for?" Zevesh asked.

"Some hot guy."

"Why are you looking for a hot guy?"

"His body and face are important to me," she said. "Plus, he needs to have a good job."

This girl was looking for trouble.

"Listen, sweetie, someone who has a good job and who is hot will not have a hard time picking up girls," Zevesh said. "Why do you think he's going to want you? What do you have that's different from other girls?"

"What do you mean?" she asked.

"What do you have that's different from other girls?" he repeated. "Do you have three boobs?"

"What the fuck are you talking about?" she asked.

"Why aren't you looking for somebody normal, who will love you for who you are?" he asked. "Then he'll care about you. When he comes home, he won't be drunk. When he comes home, he can bring you one rose—not a five hundred dollar bouquet—one rose, yellow or red. And he will come home and he will sit with you and tell you what he did all day. He'll have a glass of wine with you. You will always know that when he's done working, he'll come home to you. Is that not a better life?"

"You're right, but . . ." she paused to collect her thoughts. "That's a problem because . . .."

The cab was stopped at a red light and a couple walked by holding hands. A young boy bounded around them.

"Look at that," Zevesh said. "She looks like a normal girl. He's normal. They're holding hands and walking together. And this girl is going to be very happy with him because he loves her for who she is. She loves him for who he is. If you're looking for hot guys or hot girls, it'll never work out."

"How many guys did you date until today?" Zevesh asked her.

"Maybe six or seven," she said.

"You've had sex with six or seven guys."

"Yes."

"But you don't fit with them?"

"No."

"That's the problem," he said. "With money you can buy a one million-dollar house and a car, you can have a chauffeur and a chef. But you'll never feed your soul with this. If somebody cares about you, you could buy a two hundred-dollar dress or you can shop at K-Mart. They'll love who you are."

They sat quietly for the rest of the ride. When he pulled up to her apartment building, she gave Zevesh her card along with money for the fare.

"Call me sometime," she said. "E-mail me. I'd like to talk."

"No," he said. "You're so materialistic, and I'm not into these things, so we can't work out together as friends."

"Oh my God, you think that?" she cried.

"I'm very honest and I'm telling you to your face," Zevesh replied. "Try to be normal, then you'll see how much people love you and care about you."

Like this girl, there are too many dreamers in New York, Zevesh believes. The waiters are all actors who have never been in a TV show, a movie or even a music video. They're just dreaming, waiting for some industry bigwig to walk into the restaurant, say "you're so hot!" and make them a star.

Zevesh used to dream, but learned to be realistic and work hard from his father. His father, a university professor, brought his wife and children to Lincoln, Nebraska, from India, but Zevesh stayed behind and lived with his grandmother. When she passed away, Zevesh joined his family in the United States. He was seventeen, and his father asked him to get a job as a paperboy. The job embarrassed Zevesh. In India, his grandmother paid servants to do work. Here, his family had a nice house and a nice car and people recognized him as a professor's son. He was ashamed to be a paper boy.

He told this to his father, who said he understood. The next day, Zevesh's father took him to meet his friend Mr. Jason, a man who owned his own business and plenty of property. Afterwards, Zevesh and his father went out to lunch. A young man stopped mopping the floors to say hello to Zevesh's father. When the young man went back to mopping, Zevesh's father told him the kid was Mr. Jason's son.

"He's doing this job and not feeling any shame because he wants to stand on his feet," Zevesh's father said.

Friendships

It's not just lovers who hurt each other, but also friends. A man hailed Zevesh. As he pulled over, he saw the man hugging a crying woman.

"Buddy," Zevesh said once the man got in the cab. "I hope you didn't break her heart."

"No, she's my good friend," he replied.

"Good friend or friend with benefits?" Zevesh asked.

The man laughed.

"No, she's just my good friend."

"So is something wrong?" Zevesh asked. "Why's she crying?"

"Because she's an actor."

"Well, why then is she crying?" Zevesh pressed.

"I'm a producer, and I got her a hard job. A one-minute-thirty-second spot in a movie," he said.

Zevesh didn't understand. "And she's not happy?"

"Well, she's going to be a stripper in the movie," the guy said.

Now it was clear.

"Okay, so if you're her friend, why do you let them do that to her?"

Zevesh asked. "If you're really her good friend, you tell her that she doesn't have to strip in the movie. Showing her body for one minute thirty seconds isn't going to take her anyplace—not even *Playboy*."

The guy became quiet.

"What do you mean?"

"My friend, you're supposed to stop her!" Zevesh said. "You could give her any small role—she could be a housecleaner, anything—but you give her this role."

"What's wrong with this role?" he asked.

"This role's not for her!" Zevesh said. "That's why she has tears in eyes. Her eyes are so sad."

New Yorkers, Zevesh mused. So many rarely take the time to think. It's like they don't want to understand.

A THIN RED DRESS

~

Grant Stoddard's girlfriend leaned over and whispered into his ear. "We're going to have a night of it, and it's going to be anything you want."

They were at Grant's favorite restaurant, the Japanese hibachi chain Benihana. The sweat glistened on their cocktail glasses. The July day was hot and muggy, and Grant kept touching the clingy, single-ply material of Annisa's red wrap-around dress. The material was thin enough that he could see she wasn't wearing any underwear or bra. The slit up the dress' thigh gave Grant an excellent view of Annisa's smooth skin when she crossed her legs.

Grant knew most New Yorkers would rather spit on a chain restaurant than eat there. If out-of-town guests suggested dining at the Olive Garden, Grant would have insisted on taking them to an authentic Italian joint, complete with Sicilian grandmothers slaving in the kitchen. He would rather drown in the East River than set foot in an Applebee's. But despite his trappings of cool—he played in a band, wrote a column about sex, lived in an illegal East Village sublet, and wore skinny jeans before almost anyone—he couldn't help but love Benihana's onion volcano.

The cook came to their table and entertained them by juggling sharp kitchen tools. Grant and Annisa cheered as the cook created the famed onion volcano before tossing chopped onions and peppers on the sizzling grill. The oil spit and the cubed steak and fresh shrimp hissed as it hit the hot metal.

After the meal, she went to the restroom and Grant followed her. In the deserted hallway, she pulled up her dress so he could see her bare ass.

"You know what I'd like to do to you right now?" he said softly, knowing she loved hearing his British accent that close to her ear.

It was the perfect night. There was a guy throwing shrimp and steak and noodles around, and his girlfriend didn't have any underwear on.

"I can't wait to get you home," Grant whispered to Annisa as they left the restaurant and hopped in a cab.

"Fourteenth and C, please," said Grant.

The cabbie, a middle-aged man from the Indian subcontinent, nodded. He was listening to BBC World News on the radio.

Within seconds, they hit gridlock going downtown. Grant groaned. It should have been a six- or seven-minute cab ride home, at which point he planned on racing up the stairs and tossing Annisa onto his bed. But the traffic was hardly moving. He caught Annisa looking at him. He knew she wanted to have some fun. He put his hand on her thigh.

Raising one eyebrow, Annisa reached over and unzipped his pants. Grant was sitting behind the driver, something he preferred. That way, the driver couldn't see exactly what went on.

Annisa began messing around, and Grant relaxed, expecting a blow-job. He had received plenty of them in taxis. In the past, he used cabs as a litmus test for how adventurous girls were. If a girl got off on the idea of messing around in a taxicab, he figured it would be a good starting point for an overall fun relationship. Every single one of his girlfriends had gone down on him in a cab after a night on the town. He just thought of it as foreplay for what would come once they got home.

To his surprise, Annisa crawled on top of him, straddling his lap. He ran his hands slowly up her side and over her small chest. He could feel everything, the slant of her waist, her rib cage, almost every mole, through her thin dress. He kissed her deeply. Usually she was naked when they got in this position, but the fact that she was still wearing that flame-colored dress turned him on even more.

The traffic had barely started to move. Grant vaguely thought that something must have caused this mess of cars—maybe the president was in town, maybe it was the San Gennaro Festival—but that line of thought disappeared as he put his hands on Annisa's thighs and moved her skirt up to her waist.

She scooched up against him. She was tall, and to keep her head from bumping the ceiling, she leaned over Grant's shoulder and rested it on the parcel shelf.

She moved over him.

They barely made a sound. Annisa kept her movement to a minimum, teasing him. When the traffic started to move a bit faster, she became more animated.

Grant hoped the cab driver didn't mind, but that train of thought left his mind in short order.

Grant's hands traveled over Annisa's body, under her dress. Her hands pressed into his shoulders. It was odd seeing people sit in cars two feet away from them. To most people, it looked like Annisa was sitting on Grant's lap and they were making out. When Annisa kissed Grant's neck, he would watch the people watching them. Seconds later, as traffic moved forward, their neighbors would be gone, replaced by different cars.

The watching eyes made Grant hotter. They were only halfway home, and he still had time. He rested his hands on her hips. Traffic had slowed again and her movements became more discreet. An SUV pulled up next to them. The person in the passenger seat looked into the cab, and saw Annisa's skirt up around her waist. One second later, everyone in the SUV had moved to look on the window into Grant and Annisa's cab. They gawked. A few minutes later, the SUV crawled on.

Annisa's sexual appetite attracted him to her. She was always in the mood, something Grant relished in the few months they had been together. They had a lot of fun together, and she had few inhibitions. Her fatal flaw: She wasn't that bright. She was without a doubt the least intelligent person Grant had ever dated. He sensed that this night of *carte blanche*—not that she would recognize the French term—was some kind of last-ditch effort on her part to keep them together. She could feel him getting bored.

But right there, in the taxi, Grant was not bored. As traffic returned to normal and they neared their destination, he had eyes only for Annisa.

A few blocks away from his apartment, Annisa climbed off.

"Oh my God, I can't believe we just did that!" she said.

Neither of them had had sex in a cab before, although Grant did have sex once on the subway. They both agreed it was one for the books.

Grant left the driver a generous tip.

"I was fairly certain that he knew what was going on, and I wanted to let him know that I knew that he knew, you know?"

"I probably gave him five or six dollars on top, just to keep him sweet."

GENEROSITY

~

Larry Werther* finished his last drink at his neighborhood gay bar, the Tool Box. He felt tired and decided to call it an early night and walk home. He only lived a couple of blocks away from this Upper East Side hole-in-the-wall, anyway. Most weekends he started the party at the Tool Box and then would take a cab to a different bar on the west side, where he would have a few more drinks and maybe meet a guy. But not tonight. Tonight, his mind was on his bed.

He stood up from the bar stool and walked outside. There was a yellow cab parked by the bar. The driver sitting inside was handsome. He had dark hair and eyes, and from what Larry could tell, his figure seemed trim. He looked good, and dark men were just Larry's type. Larry thought he caught the driver checking him out.

Larry decided to bide his time. He pulled out a pack of cigarettes and lit one. When he looked up, he saw the driver staring at him, smiling.

Barry returned his smile.

"Hi," he said.

The cabbie got an eager look on his face.

"Hi, can I take you somewhere?"

Larry decided to go to the west side after all. He refused to officially acknowledge the voice in the back of his head wishing for something good to happen—possibly with the cab driver—but the voice was there.

"Okay," Larry said.

He walked up to the driver and put out his hand. The driver shook it, holding it a bit longer than he should have.

"I'm Rajiv," he said.

"I'm Larry."

They got in the cab, Larry in the back seat.

"So where are you going?"

Larry gave him the address of a gay bar on the west side.

They started talking. The driver asked Larry about his job (magazine editor) and where he lived (Upper East Side). Larry asked him how long he was a cab driver and how he liked his job.

They continued with the small talk.

"Where are you from?" Larry asked.

"India," the driver answered.

"Oh, really? That's great because I find Indian men very sexy."

"Well, that's good," the driving said, smiling into the rearview mirror. "Would you like to come sit up front with me?"

"Of course."

The cab didn't have a partition, so at the next red light, Larry climbed over the seat, a move he found more subtle than getting out of the car and running to the front.

Rajiv drove and they talked. The driver kept his eyes on the road, took one hand off the wheel and unzipped his pants. Larry unzipped his own pants and reached over. Rajiv drove slowly, but not so slowly as to attract attention.

To mix it up, Larry leaned over and went to work on Rajiv. Rajiv groaned and pressed on the gas. After a few minutes, Larry was ready to sit back up and take a breather. But just then a semi truck pulled up behind them, his lights shining into the cab. Panicked by the lights, Rajiv pushed Larry's head back down, gagging him and holding him in place.

"Someone could see," he explained, while Larry choked.

The truck passed, and Larry lifted his head up. They weren't too far from his west side destination. After choking on Rajiv, Larry had enough of him, and decided to speed things up. He went to town on Rajiv, employing his sure-fire move.

Rajiv quickly got worked up, and after a minute was practically lifting off the seat.

"You have to stop, you have to stop, you have to stop!" Rajiv yelled.

Larry stopped. He chalked Rajiv's excitement up to being uncircumcised. In Larry's experience, uncircumcised men were always much more sensitive than circumcised men.

"Do you want to do more?" Rajiv asked.

Larry thought for a minute, and decided why not. He wasn't in the mood for a bar anymore.

"OK, but you have to take me home after that."

"How about Central Park?" Rajiv suggested, pulling over on Central Park West.

"I'm going to leave my meter running," he added.

Larry couldn't figure out why the hell he'd leave his meter running, but didn't feeling like arguing.

"Alright," he said.

It was after midnight, and they only had to walk a short ways into the park before the darkness covered them. They started messing around again. But this time around, Rajiv didn't want to touch Larry, but he wanted to be touched.

Although he suspected it all along, at this point Larry would have put money on the fact that Rajiv was married and had kids. He never looked for a wedding ring, and he never wanted to ask, but felt he didn't need to. He trusted his gut instincts. An Indian guy in his mid-to-late thirties, driving a cab in New York City? He would almost have to be married, unless he was gay.

And Larry never thought Rajiv was gay. There weren't the typical signs—he seemed decidedly masculine, from the way he held himself to the way he dressed and talked.

Another sure indicator of Rajiv's heterosexuality, at least in Larry's mind, was how he acted when they were hooking up. It was all about Rajiv's pleasure, which is what would happen if a straight guy were with a gay guy, Larry suspected. Larry figured he was just a married guy with kids who had an opportunity to have some sex. Rajiv played the man's role in the process, so he didn't think about it as gay.

That's a common thing in some countries, Larry read, and certainly not unheard of in America. He heard numerous stories about men doing exactly what Rajiv did—men whose sexual experimentation never tarnished their reputations as lady killers.

"You want to do it?" Rajiv asked.

Larry wasn't really in the mood, but didn't want to say so. Instead, he consented. But once they started, he couldn't get into it. They were in the middle of a park. It wasn't comfortable. It wasn't working.

"We have to stop," he said.

Rajiv begged him to keep going, but Larry stood firm. They got back into the car.

"You should sit in back," Rajiv said, "so it doesn't look suspicious."

"Sure," said Larry, noting wryly that Rajiv didn't seem to care about what looked "suspicious" earlier.

"Where do you want me to take you?" Rajiv asked.

"Ninety-sixth and Second Avenue."

Larry knew he only had fifteen dollars in his wallet, but he figured Rajiv would only ask him for five dollars or so. Why wouldn't he? In Larry's mind, it should be a free ride—pun intended—as they both had their fun. He figured he could leave the remaining ten dollars as a generous tip.

Rajiv pulled up to Larry's apartment. Larry spoke first.

"Well, the meter says fifteen dollars, but hopefully you'll be more generous," he teased.

"More generous?" Rajiv replied indignantly. "I thought I did you the favor!"

Larry's expression turned to surprised confusion.

"Oh, come on, come on!"

"Didn't you enjoy that?" Rajiv pushed. "Wasn't that nice?"

"Yes, but I could get that at any gay bar in New York City—for free!" Larry cried.

Sick of arguing and in the mood for bed, Larry relented.

"Alright, but I honestly only have fifteen dollars on me."

"Can you get more money?"

Larry stared at him. The guy was out of control, he thought. And to think that Rajiv picked him up at the bar! It was unreal. First he shoved Larry's head down, choking him. Then he insisted on having sex in the park, even when Larry wasn't in the mood. And now Rajiv had the audacity to ask for more money! Larry worked his anger into a lather. It would have cost him just a bit more to have more drinks in a bar!

But he kept his anger bottled up inside. He never thought of not paying Rajiv, or of telling him to fuck off.

Larry got out of the cab and walked to the corner bodega, where he took out cash from the ATM. He went back to the cab and handed Rajiv thirty dollars—twice the fare.

"That's all?" Rajiv asked.

"I think that's more than generous," Larry said, turning his back and walking away.

CHAPTER 7

CULTURE CRASH

Race, Religion, and Confrontation

In a city where nearly 170 languages are spoken and 36 percent of the population was born outside the United States, issues surrounding race are a consistent, complex theme underlying many relationships, including that between taxi driver and passenger.

Race is often the most apparent difference between driver and passenger. But socio-economic discrepancies from either side of the partition can also play into racial stereotypes. Yellow cabs primarily serve Manhattan—one of the wealthiest counties in the United States, where the weekly wage averaged $2,805 in early 2008, according to the New York Bureau of Labor Statistics. Cabbies tend to live in the outer boroughs, like Queens, where the average person brings home $852 each week. Now add the fact that 90 percent of drivers are foreign born, as compared with only 29 percent of Manhattanites. These discrepancies in income and background lead to a physical and mental separation of worlds—a separation that can lead to a lack of understanding.

When it comes to race, it's hardly a secret that black men have trouble catching cabs. A number of cabbies I spoke with made comments—some hedged, some not—revealing their belief that black men were more likely than other passengers to mug them, stiff them the fare, or instruct them to drive to dangerous neighborhoods. Even drivers who adamantly claimed to pick up anyone needing a ride shook their head in sympathy for African-Americans, admitting they knew others who avoided picking up blacks.

In the shadow of 9/11, the topic of race swung away from black passengers and towards Muslim drivers. In the United States, reports issued by Humans Rights Watch showed that reported violence against people who appeared to be Muslims skyrocketed after the attacks. In New York and around the country, mosques were defaced, anonymous threatening phone calls targeted Muslim organizations, and reports of harassment and physical assault against Muslims jumped.

More than half of New York's taxi drivers were born in Muslim countries, and these drivers felt—and some still feel—intensely vulnerable. With drivers' names listed on the hack licenses that hang on the partition, passengers can easily identify those named Muhammad or Khalid as having a Muslim background.

After the attacks, some passengers showed drivers empathy; others didn't. One driver told me a passenger joked about tossing a lit match into his cab's gas tank. In another story, a passenger told me how he and his drunk friends were in a cab trying to find a party downtown, near the wreckage of the World Trade Center. When the driver couldn't find the site, one of the passengers exploded at him, saying, "Why not? Your people blew it up!" before collapsing into drunken giggles.

Because their turbans reminded Americans of Osama bin Laden, Sikh drivers feared being targets of violence. After 9/11, many Sikh drivers posted a paper on the back of their cab's partition explaining the Sikh religion, it's origin in northern India and its commonalities with Buddhism as an attempt to ward of potential threats.

In city as diverse as New York, the combinations of racial conflict seem endless. What happens when an Indian gets in a cab driven by a Pakistani or Bengali? How do the rules of interaction change when a

Vietnamese woman gets in a cab driven by a Chinese man? Festering wounds, blood rivalries and predilections nurtured by generations of repression don't disappear when you step into a cab.

HUFFED

~

O n Barry Heckard's second night as a taxi driver, traffic slowed to a stop while driving through Greenwich Village at about midnight. On Christopher between Seventh Avenue and Bleecker, a black man walked up to his open window.

"Hi. I don't have any money, but you're going to take me to the East Village."

The man wasn't asking. He seemed a little drunk.

Barry was twenty-one years old, slight, blond and effete. The man's gruff attitude frightened him.

"Today, I would have told him to take a fucking hike. But back then, being so young and naïve and scared, I just said okay."

Barry had been in Manhattan for all of two months. He had felt drawn to New York, and had transferred from Long Island University to a college in the city.

He shared an apartment with a friend, and decided to become a taxi driver. He'd never done anything like it before. He figured he could make good money and set his own hours. Plus, Barry wanted to experience "city life,"—the food, the bars, the people—and what's more city than driving a cab?

Barry had left all of his doors unlocked. Foregoing the back seat, the man walked over to the passenger door, opened it and got in.

"Ah . . ." Barry began.

The man's behavior freaked him out, but he didn't want to go head-to-head with the guy. He took some comfort in the man's unassuming pants and shirt. At least he didn't look like a gangster. Barry let it go.

"I'm going to Second and B," the guy said.

Barry nodded his head and drove off. Along the way, the man took out a white handkerchief and bottle filled with a clear liquid. The man opened the bottle, put the handkerchief over the bottle top, turned it upside down and then righted it. He then put the handkerchief over his face and loudly inhaled.

After breathing in the stuff, the guy muttered gibberish, got lightheaded and briefly passed out, his head lolling on the seat, before popping back up to alertness.

Barry had no idea what was in the bottle, and had never heard of inhaling to get high, but it didn't take a rocket scientist to figure that's what this guy was doing.

All Barry wanted to do was get to the East Side so he could dump him out of the cab.

The man put his handkerchief over the top of the bottle again, flipped it, then put the cloth up to his face, inhaling. Once again, he uttered nonsensical phrases—louder than last time—before briefly passing out.

Barry drove further east and the man took repeated huffs from the cloth. Each time, his voice got louder, carrying out the windows unrolled on the hot summer day. Sometimes the man sang. But whatever he did, he never made any sense—in fact, his comments became more off-the-wall. The man blanked out briefly a few additional times.

He seemed to have forgotten about Barry.

"It was like I wasn't there most of the ride, which was good," Barry said. "I was more than happy that he didn't pay much attention to me."

Unfortunately, once they got to Houston Street, close to their destination, his passenger remembered Barry existed.

His passenger also felt like sharing.

The guy took the cloth, this time giving it an extra-generous douse of the clear liquid. The handkerchief in his right hand, the man reached over and tried to push the cloth onto Barry's face while they were stopped at a red light. Barry, his foot on the brake, used both his arms to fight the bigger man off.

"No! No!" Barry yelled. "I don't want it! I don't want it!"

But the man didn't care. The man muttered as he shifted his weight, forcing himself on top of Barry. Barry knew he had to keep the guy off him. He shielded his face with his arms. But the cloth seemed to come closer and closer to his face. Barry's couldn't defend himself with his legs—it was imperative his foot stay on the brake.

The man twisted to the left. He wedged himself between Barry and the steering wheel, and used all his weight to push the cloth towards Barry's face. The man's legs kicked. Barry could see the veins popping on the guy's face. Barry tried to twist away from him, but he was held fast. He was using all his strength to keep the guy off of him, but his slender arms were no match for the weight of the man's entire body, pressing down.

Grunting with exertion, the drug addict forced the handkerchief down over Barry's mouth and nose. Barry held his breath.

One second.

Two seconds.

Three seconds.

Barry struggled. He couldn't get the hand away.

Four seconds.

Five seconds.

His foot was still on the brake. His heart raced. The man's face was inches from his own. He refused to inhale. Barry gave a huge final push, forcing the hand away from his face.

The man got off him and leaned back in his own seat. Maybe he assumed Barry inhaled the cloth. Or maybe he was sick of fighting. Maybe he wanted more for himself.

Barry stuck his head outside the window, gulping in the fresh air.

His passenger took a massive whiff off the rag. He let out a huge roar. The man continued screaming and Barry was afraid someone would hear him through the open windows and assume Barry was attacking him.

Two blocks later, Barry arrived at the destination.

He looked over.

The man was out cold.

Barry took a deep breath. How the hell was he going to get this druggie out of his cab? It was only his second day of work! He decided to try and wake him.

"Buddy, you gotta get up," Barry said. "You gotta get up."

He wasn't getting up.

Barry turned the cab off. He grabbed everything that was important—his keys, his change dispenser, and the written log he kept of pick-ups and drop-offs that he had to turn it in at the end of the evening. He got out of the cab and walked to the nearest payphone, about a block away. Fortunately, it was in working order. He dialed 911.

"911, what's your emergency?" said the voice on the other end of the line.

"I've got this guy passed out in my cab," Barry said. "He won't get up and he's doing drugs."

"Alright, where are you?" the operator asked.

"I'm at Second Street and Avenue B."

"We'll send someone right over," the operator replied.

Barry hung up the phone and waited a short ways from the cab, in case the man woke up and became irate. Then he saw a cop car driving towards him. He ran into the street, waving his arms for them to stop. They stopped.

He looked at his cab.

The windshield was smashed, crack marks spread across it like a spider web. It looked like a fist slammed into the glass. The man was no longer in the car.

"Shit!" Barry thought.

He looked up the street and saw the man calmly walking away. He had only made it half a block.

The two cops had gotten out of the car.

Barry was in a panic.

"That guy over there just broke my windshield, he was doing drugs in my car, and he wouldn't pay me anything," he said, speaking quickly to the cops and pointing at the man ambling down the street.

"We'll go talk to him. You just stay there," the cops said.

They walked over to the man, and started talking. After a few minutes, one cop came back over to Barry, while the other cop stayed with the man.

"Did you see him do it?" the cop asked. "Did you see him break the windshield?"

"Why, what did he say?" Barry asked.

"He says he didn't do it."

"Well, he definitely did it."

"Did you see him do it?" the cop asked again.

"Well, no," Barry truthfully answered. "I was on the phone calling 911."

"You know, if you didn't see him do it, there's nothing we can do," the cop said.

Barry didn't know what to do. The guy had clearly smashed the windshield with his fist. No one else was around. No one else could have done it. He even believed the guy was messed up enough that he could have broken the glass and promptly forgotten about it. Why couldn't they just arrest him?

The cop wasn't done with Barry.

"Listen," the cop said. "That's why you never trust a nigger. You never let them in your cab, because they're nothing but trouble."

THE TELL-TALE NOSE RING

~

A long night of dancing turned Shaheen Pasha's calves to rubber and her sweaty shirt stuck to her stomach. For the past three hours, she and her friends had grooved to the sounds of Indian dance music, just as they did the first Thursday of every month at the Basement Bhangra party held at the club, S.O.B.'s.

By 2:30 a.m., she wanted to go home. She had a 10 a.m. class at Manhattan's Pace University the next morning. The first of her group to leave, she began making her goodbyes.

"Are you going to be OK going home by yourself?" her friend Leena asked.

"I'll be fine," Shaheen said. "I'll take a cab."

She left the club, sweating enough to leave her leather jacket unbuttoned in the chilly March air. She found a taxi directly outside the club and climbed in.

"Hi, I'm going to the corner of Spruce and Gold," she said.

The cabbie, who, like Shaheen's family emigrated from the Indian subcontinent, glanced at her through the rear-view mirror, then grinned at the sight of her long black hair, large almond eyes and tight, red sleeveless shirt.

He pulled away from the curb, but seemed more interested in checking out Shaheen's chest through the mirror than watching the road. Shaheen pulled her jacket together.

"How are you?" he asked. She didn't answer.

"Where are you from?" She was, in fact, from Brooklyn, and her parents were from Pakistan, but she had no intention of answering him. She met his questions with silence.

Undaunted, he tried again. "How are you doing?"

Shaheen crossed her legs, looked out the window, and kept her mouth shut. She already knew the routine. Late at night, South Asian cab drivers frequently hit on her, identifying her as one of their own because of her nose ring and dark hair. Having grown up in Brooklyn's rough East New York neighborhood in the gang-infested 1980s, she knew how to act tough and stand firm, making herself seem much larger than only five feet tall. So when taxi drivers pushed too much, she felt no guilt about ignoring them.

"Are you Indian? Are you Pakistani? What are you?" the cabbie continued, his questions coming rapid fire as he stopped for a red light.

She glanced at him—he looked to be in his mid-thirties. He leered back at her. She shifted uncomfortably. Diverting her eyes, Shaheen looked at his hack license posted on the back of the clear divider between herself the driver and saw his last name was Singh, a name she associated with Punjabis.

"What do you do? Where do you go to school? Do you go to school?" he asked, barely taking a breath, his questions spilling into each other.

His eyes focused more intently on her than before. Shaheen looked out the other window. They had reached the financial district, where she lived. The streets looked desolate. By day, Shaheen couldn't walk one block without running into scores of Wall Street types wearing designer suits and Italian leather shoes, but this late at night the only living things Shaheen noticed were the cabbie, the occasional homeless person and the rats.

Finally, her dorm came into view. The cab driver turned onto Spruce, but instead of slowing down he sped up.

"Stop! Stop!" Shaheen said. "This is my stop right here!"

"Well, we had such a nice conversation, I figured we could talk some more," he answered in an amicable voice, continuing down the road.

Shaheen saw his meter was off. "No, I need to go home!" she yelled.

"There's an all night-diner, I figured we could go get a coffee," he continued, driving past the next street.

Shaheen's mother's voice ran through her head, the lecture a familiar and oft-repeated one: "Don't take cabs by yourself late at night," she scolded in her Indian accent. "It's a closed space. It's not safe."

"Let me out of here!" Shaheen screamed.

"No, no, you're fine," he cooed, gunning for a green light.

The light changed to red, and the driver slowed. Shaheen grabbed her purse, lunged for the door handle, slammed the door open and threw herself out of the car, landing on her feet. She sprinted towards her dorm in her platform heels, barely slowing after she swung through her front door, only stopping when she saw the security guard. Feeling safer, she peeked outside to make sure the driver didn't attempt to chase her by making a U-turn and driving the wrong way up her one-way street.

He hadn't.

BLACK AND WHITE

~

Whenever Sean Croix*, a black man, had to hail a cab, he had his white friends do it. He would hide around the corner or behind a light, darting into the backseat at the last moment. His friend Ted Boss*, also African-American, did too. Both moved to New York ten years ago to attend Columbia University's medical school. Sean, who grew up in Miami, knew New York cabbies' reputation for racism; Ted, who came from San Antonio, had no clue. Today, both have countless stories—all told with a residue of anger—illustrating their struggle to catch cabs.

Sean once called a car service to pick him up at his Park Slope apartment. The driver took one look at him and sped past—not even slowing when Sean ran down the street after him. Sean recognized the problem. Not only was he African-American, but he was wearing an oversized Miami sweatshirt with his hood up. In other words, he was dressed like a black man who probably didn't hang out in ritzy Park Slope.

In another incident, Ted and his girlfriend were heading to a club in the chic Meatpacking district. When Ted, who favors designer clothes and Italian leather shoes, went to hail an oncoming cab, the cabbie immediately switched on his off-duty light. But when Ted's girlfriend Nina, who has pale blonde hair and fair skin, stepped into the street beside him, the cab pulled to a stop, asked Nina their destination, and let them into the car. Nina, who until this point considered Ted rather paranoid in his sensitivity regarding cabs, could hardly believe the blatant racism she witnessed.

Listening to their struggles, you get the impression that a successful cab hail for Sean and Ted is a feat comparable to your average Joe climbing Mount Everest. And as mountain climbers take years to train, learning from their mistakes, Ted and Sean developed their own offensive strategies—especially necessary when they roomed together in Washington Heights, a high-crime neighborhood taxicabs actively avoided. They dressed up, leaving the hoodies at home. They tried hailing cabs on different streets. They had white friends hail cabs. In desperate times, they convinced white strangers on the street to help them get a taxi.

The relationship between taxis and black men has multiple layers, and is fed by a number of issues, including racism, fear of crime, and economics. Even President Barack Obama has referenced New York's racist cabbies. During the August 2007 YouTube Democratic primary debate on CNN, when asked if he was black enough, Obama replied, "You know, when I'm catching a cab in Manhattan . . . I think I've given my credentials."

Most cab drivers themselves are minorities. About half of New York's cabbies come from Muslim nations, with a large number from India and the Caribbean. Some argue that immigrant cabbies have internalized white prejudice. It is true, after all, that many American films exported to developing nations portray black communities as isolated and violent.

More weighty is the fact that driving is a dangerous job. Hacks carry large amounts of cash and have their backs to strangers they pick up off the streets. Many drivers can tell terrifying stories of guns held to their heads or knives to their throats. And many cabbies just can't shake the notion that black men are more likely to rob them than other passengers.

Dinesh D'Souza spoke to a number of cab drivers while researching his book, *The End of Racism*. The drivers told him that although the job required them to pick up all hails, if they felt it was a choice between their personal safety or receiving a ticket for bypassing a perceived shady pedestrian, they'd take the ticket. Every time.

Another reason is economic. One night after watching taxi after taxi pass him by before one finally stopped, Ted asked his cab driver, an African-American, why cabs wouldn't pick him up. The driver gave Ted the money talk. Many black men in New York live in the far reaches of Brooklyn or the Bronx, he explained. After dropping their clients off, this meant twenty minutes of driving and guzzling gas—generally without a fare—to get back to Manhattan. They simply couldn't afford to leave the borough that often.

Numerous cabbies I spoke with flat-out said they don't stop for black men. Some mentioned fear of a hold-up, others said they'd been stiffed by black men in the past. One cabbie, a white guy who always stops for black men, shook his head in empathy at the fact that African-Americans often feel compelled to wave a twenty-dollar bill in the air to get cabs to stop.

The problem reached a publicity zenith in 1999 after *Lethal Weapon's* Danny Glover, frustrated at his repeated inability to catch a cab, filed a formal complaint with the TLC. The media jumped on the story.

Spurred on by the national embarrassment, New York's government implemented 'Operation Refusal.' They planted black undercover officers to act as pedestrians needing cabs. If a cab drove by a black agent but stopped for a white agent half a block later, it meant trouble for the driver.

Some African-Americans have reported that in recent years the problem has improved. *New York Times* writer Calvin Sims said as much in his October 15, 2006 article "An Arm in the Air for that Cab Ride Home."

But Ted and Sean don't see a difference. And although both have been in New York for more than ten years, neither has gotten used to it. Today, they both work at hospitals, meaning they have an additional fear—what if they need to rush to work because of a medical emergency, but no cabs will stop? What then?

"When you get resigned and you get complacent, it means to accept," said Sean, stressing each word, letting you feel its weight. "You never accept. You never get complacent. You're never resigned to it. You get upset each and every time like it's the first time."

Ted nodded in agreement.

"It means that something you should be able to take for granted you can't," he said. "I still get pissed."

While there is no obvious solution, Sean has found something of an answer to the problem.

"Now that I'm married to a white girl, I get cabs all the time!"

HASSLED

~

"It's no fun riding in a cab if you can't hassle the cab driver," Anthony Romano* said. "You're putting your life in their hands—an immigrant with no regard for the traffic laws of this country."

He claimed to be joking.

"Cabbies are bad news," he continued. "They're not the best drivers. And if they were super-successful people, they probably would have moved on from this career by the time I got in the cab," he added.

Why would that be?

"Because almost anything is better than that job, and there's no money in that."

At this point, Anthony confessed to having also driven a cab, but only for two weeks. He never bothered to follow through and get his hack license. As a professed life-long New Yorker—he was born at Manhattan's St. Vincent's hospital on Seventh Avenue and Thirteenth Street—he's no immigrant, a fact immediately recognizable by his thick New York accent. One wonders if he has much regard for the traffic laws of this country.

"I just want to get them to loosen up and not kill me," he said about trading jabs with cabbies.

It was in October 2001 that Anthony found himself, once again, hassling his cab driver in a "good-natured way."

Here's the setting: New Yorkers were in a state of shock. Terrorists transformed the Twin Towers into a five-story-high mass grave of twisted metal and smoking rubble. Rescue and recovery missions continued, but it was clear that there would be no more survivors and very few remains for families to bury. Huge swaths of the city smelled like burning plastic. People living near downtown regularly blew black funk from their noses. Employees at New York's *NBC News* and the *New York Post* found an envelope filled with anthrax in their mailroom, and in mid-October, someone sent anthrax to two Democratic senators. Paranoia was high.

During the aftermath of 9/11 Anthony and his buddy, Joey, left a bar on the east side of Manhattan. The time was 3 a.m., and they had been drinking all night.

"I was in no condition to drive, let's put it that way," he said.

They hailed a cab, climbed in, and told the driver they were heading to Astoria, Queens.

Anthony readied for his game.

He looked at the driver and decided he was Muslim—a wild stab in the dark. He could possibly have figured out if the driver was Muslim by looking at his name—Muhammad? Abdul?—on the hack license hanging on the partition, but frankly, Anthony was too messed up to read. Yet his decision had been made, and his assumption that the driver was Muslim influenced Anthony's line of questioning.

"Hey, man, what's with the anthrax?" he asked.

Anthony claims he did this good-naturedly, as opposed to aggressively. He's a happy drunk, he alleged.

"I don't know," the cabbie answered in an unperturbed voice.

"What's the problem, man?" Anthony continued.

"I don't know," repeated the driver, a thin man with sunken eyes. "I've been here for fifteen years. I don't know."

Anthony didn't give up his needling so easily.

"But what's the issue, dude?" he asked.

"I don't know, I'm from Egypt," the driver responded.

"Oh yeah?" Anthony said. "I've been to Egypt. I saw the pyramids. They were cool."

This was a line of bullshit. He'd never been there. Anthony insists that he normally never lies to cabbies, but for some reason, he did this time. The driver believed him, and they had a talk about Egypt. It wasn't the deepest conversation, probably because he was so wasted.

Ten minutes into the ride, as they approached the Queensboro Bridge, the driver asked them, "Hey, you guys smoke?"

Joey chimed in for the first time.

"Yeah, we smoke whatever," he said.

Relief washed over Anthony at his friend's quick response. He hadn't known how to answer the question, but Joey came up with the right answer. Joey could be counted on for being sharp.

"Have you ever smoked hash?" the driver asked.

"No," Joey said. "But we'll try it."

The driver reached down, pulled out a joint, and lit it up. He inhaled, and handed it back through the open partition. Anthony and his friend took a hit. The joint looked like a normal joint—it wasn't massive like one rolled by Cheech & Chong— but it was strong, according to Anthony. He had never smoked anything like it.

They passed the joint around, and Anthony had the "mellowest" ride over the Queensboro Bridge of his life.

"It was totally wicked awesome," he added.

Then the paranoia kicked in.

"I am the paranoid type," Anthony confesses. "That's just standard for me. It doesn't relate to my drug habits. It's standard New Yorker paranoia drilled into me by years of living in a way-too-multicultural city. It's sensory overload. It's crowded, it's dirty, really big swaths of the city smell like urine all the time. It's normal, it's home. I don't enjoy it anywhere else, but it is ridiculous at the same time. Most cities of this size have nowhere near the demographic of New York. NYC is full of everyone. They could be from Mars. They show up, need a house and money, and we say, 'Cool, welcome aboard. Have you ever thought of a career in banking? Do you think you can sell stock? Do you have the gift of gab?' It's like the *The Hudsucker Proxy*. You ever seen it? The Coen Brothers' film? Tim Robbins is a goof. He invents the hula-hoop and he goes from the mailroom to the CEO's office in an hour. It's the Horatio Alger story. That's New York. 'Hello, we have a mailroom for you, and you're welcome.'"

The paranoia increased because Anthony could not control where his mind was going with these thoughts—back to the mailroom of the media outlets that received the envelopes filled with white powder.

"I was convinced that the joint was full of anthrax," Anthony admitted. "Not in a real way, but in a worse-than-real way, in a ridiculous way."

He never told the cab driver—that would have been rude—but he told his friend as the cab made its way towards Astoria.

"You're such an asshole," Joey replied, making fun of him.

Anthony didn't care. He knew that everyone standing on the street corners they drove by were opening envelopes filled with anthrax.

Then the driver got lost. It wasn't his fault—The TLC requires cabbies to know all streets in Manhattan but only key destinations in the outer boroughs. Joey had recently moved to Astoria and couldn't remember exactly where he lived. As a result, they were driving while trying to figure out where to go. In his paranoia, he was convinced that the cabbie was purposely driving in circles to run up the meter.

"We gotta get out of the cab, the guy's milking us," Anthony told Joey.

Joey simply continued making fun of Anthony's dubious mental state, but then relented, figuring they could walk home. The cabbie pulled over, but while the guys exited from the back, Anthony, lacking any motor skills, dropped the joint on the floor of the backseat. All three men started scouring the floor for the roach, the driver included.

"Looking for the joint became a big hullabaloo," Anthony said.

It was like looking for anthrax; he couldn't get away from it. Finally, the driver found it. He got back behind the wheel, and the three men exchanged pleasantries before the driver peeled off.

Left to their own devices, Anthony and Joey oriented themselves and discovered they were only three blocks from Joey's apartment.

"So far, as I can tell, there wasn't any anthrax in the joint," Anthony concluded.

He said that he came away from the experience with a newfound faith in society.

"I think that was a very important melding of the American world," he said. "It shows that we can share drugs together, and if we can do that, we can do almost everything."

Like heckle drivers who may or may not be Muslim, smoke their hash, and then flip out on them.

TOO CLOSE TO HOME

~

Lisa Brixen* ran out of her sister-in-law's Tribeca apartment into the snow. She was running late for a tax seminar in SoHo and needed to make it there on time. She hailed a taxi, got in, and told the driver her destination.

The convoluted mess of downtown streets posed a problem to many drivers in New York, but this cabbie knew how to navigate all of them. Lisa watched him weave in and out of traffic, his small, wiry frame resting in the seat. He had sensed the pattern that governed this labyrinth of streets, and he had a clear strategy to make his way though in rush hour traffic. A Zen-like quality infused his driving ability and talent.

Lisa could tell by the way he closed gaps between cars and took turns that he was tough and energetic, if not high-strung. Taking in his mocha complexion and the gray hair peppered with black, she assumed he came from the Middle East or South Asia, probably Pakistan. But it was clear he had lived in the United States for a long time—only an expert with years of practice could squeeze a cab through traffic and back roads like this. Impressed by his driving skills, and relieved that she would make it to her seminar on time, Lisa opened conversation.

"You're not one of those taxi drivers who needs the new GPS system," she said.

He laughed. "Yes, the streets of lower Manhattan are difficult to navigate," he said.

They continued discussing the twisted layout of downtown Manhattan's streets. The man said he spent a long time memorizing and learning the city, and was proud of his ability to navigate tough spots. He said that once his son had ridden with him, and that his son was also surprised at and impressed with his father's absolute knowledge of the streets and traffic. From there, the conversation naturally segued into family, and the driver told Lisa that he had four children, all of whom went to college.

Lisa kept asking questions. The man fascinated her. An avid traveler, Lisa always made a point to speak with cab drivers in the forty-plus countries she's visited, asking them their opinions about their current government, their leaders, and their opinions of the country's economic condition. She rarely spoke to cabbies in New York, but was happy she made this exception.

How Much Drivers Earn

~

Cab drivers are finally earning more than they did in 1929, after adjusting for inflation. Today, the average driver appears to earn between $126 and $152 per nine-hour shift, according to the TLC.

What happened to drivers pay between then and now? According to Schaller Consulting, newspaper articles in 1929 stated that drivers took home a bit more than $11 an hour, or $132 when adjusted for inflation. But when the Great Depression hit, drivers' incomes sank to $4 a shift in 1934. Their pay rose steadily, nearly topping the peak of 1929 in 1981, when the limited number of medallions and the unionization of drivers saw inflation-adjusted income excluding benefits reach $130 a shift.

A fare increase in 2004 had drivers pocketing $158 per shift in 2005. But skyrocketing gas prices meant that any extra cash going towards drivers' dinner tables was quickly sucked up by oil companies. So the city stepped in and implemented a substantial fare increase in 2007..

But the leasing system, implemented in the early 1980s, has left cabbies out in the cold. Under the system, cabbies pay to lease a cab for a day, instead of taking home a commission. While both lessees and commission-paid cabbies took home the same amount of cash, lessees lost out on valuable benefits, like health insurance and a pension plan. Also, lessees worked more hours than commission drivers did, meaning their hourly wage suffered.

He told her that today was his granddaughter's birthday. She was five, and they had thrown her a party that afternoon. She wore a pink dress that his wife had beaded by hand. He and his wife were both proud of her, how smart she was, and how well she was doing in kindergarten. The driver glowed when he spoke about her.

Their conversion moved onto news and current events. Lisa cracked a joke about President George W. Bush and the driver laughed.

Lisa assumed her next question was innocuous.

"So where are you from?"

The driver slammed on his brakes, yanked the steering wheel to the curb and brought the cab to a screeching halt.

"Get the hell out of my cab!" he shouted.

Lisa sat stunned.

"Why?"

"Get out now!" he screamed.

He had stopped so haphazardly that he nearly pulled the cab onto the sidewalk. The cab sat at an awkward angle, blocking the street.

Lisa sat bewildered. Then her temper slowly rose. What right did he have to yell at her? What was wrong with that question? She got out of the cab and walked up to the passenger-side window.

"Fuck you," she yelled at him. "You can't do this! You have no idea where I'm coming from. This is so unfair to freak out! Why are you yelling at me? Why don't you ask me where I'm coming from? I'm interested in other cultures, I studied geography, and I like to think about where people are from!"

"This is my country!" he shouted back. "My children were born here, my grandchildren were born here! I pay my taxes!"

Lisa's legs shook more from anger than cold. She normally walked away from confrontations with crazy people. But she couldn't believe this man would attack her after they had such an intimate conversation.

"I'm really offended!" she yelled back. "You assumed that my question had an ulterior motive. And my question was just that—a direct question. I just wanted to know where you were from!"

The driver opened his door and stepped out of the car into the snow.

"This is my country! My children were born here! My grandchildren were born here!" he said.

It was like talking to a wall. His jaw was set, his expression stubborn. He wasn't hearing her. Lisa had a longing in the pit of her stomach to make him understand what she meant. That she meant no judgment and no harm. And she needed him to understand that his reaction to her question was completely unacceptable.

"You just made some assumptions about me," she shouted. "It's really offensive to me that you'll engage in this conversation for ten minutes and then be so offended by my question."

People walking by paused to look at then. A car stuck behind the poorly parked cab began honking.

"I'm sick and tired asking people where I'm from," he said, slightly calmer but still yelling. "Why does it matter where I'm from? I have children here, I have grandchildren here, why ask where I am from?"

"What was offensive about this question?" she asked.

She thought she couldn't get any more frustrated, but now, of the two of them, she was the one losing it.

"There's no assumption in my question! I wanted to know where you're from. The question that I'm asking you is the question I'm asking you." She paused.

"I am from here!"

Lisa knew what the conversation was about. And she knew that he knew. They would never say it, but the fight was about 9/11 and the sense of belonging.

The driver just didn't seem to understand they were on the same side.

It seemed logical to her that after 9/11, plenty of passengers had asked him the same question, but they meant something by it; something anti-Muslim. And it only made sense that if anti-Muslim violence shot up in New York, and around the country, the unreported cases of harassment skyrocketed, too. He had lived in the United

States for decades. Maybe he felt that the secure home he found for his family was no longer safe.

But this didn't change the fact that her driver needed to—must—understand her. Not everyone thought that way. Sometimes a question was only a question.

"You're not listening to me, you're not listening!" she said.

More people watched hesitantly from the sidewalk. A number of cars, backed up behind the taxi, were honking. Lisa felt calmer, and the driver had inched towards where she stood near the hood. They were completely engaged.

For one moment, the driver looked slightly embarrassed. He had finally heard her! He took a few steps towards her, gave her a quick hug and released her.

"I'm from Pakistan," he said.

"I figured that," she said. "And you speak Urdu?"

"You know of Urdu?" He was surprised.

"Yes."

His frustration seemed to be gone.

Now the cars were really honking.

"You're only two blocks away," he said, quickly getting into the cab.

He pulled away. A line of angry drivers trailed after him.

Chapter 8

WELCOME TO NEW YORK, YOU &#@%!

Unsuspecting Tourists Meet Taxis

Everyone pretends that it's easy to spot a tourist, and to a certain extent, that's true. Plenty of Americans born east of the Hudson River stick out with their pleated khakis, white sneakers and broad smiles, as do the Euro-trash tourists with their aggressively highlighted hair, Prada heels and shopping bags. A third well-traveled set, generally in New York visiting friends, does blend with the locals, sharing their penchant for East Village bars, outer borough visits, and Chuck Taylors.

All these visitors have at least one thing in common—well, one thing other than a penchant for Times Square: They entertain romantic visions of New York City cabbies, formed by urban legends, television, and movies like Scorsese's *Taxi Driver* and Jarmusch's *Night on Earth*.

After questioning a small sampling of friends and family in the Midwest, many of whom had never visited New York, I learned cabbies are thought of either as white guys with cigars clamped between their teeth or immigrants with brown skin. Most respondents expected cabbies to be gruff, while a few envisioned them as men who pontificate about life. All the Midwestern respondents assumed cabbies drove like maniacs, and most assumed cabbies would cheat them out of cash.

I sampled an equally small and unreliable handful of foreign friends. They hold close some of the same stereotypes about cabbies, assuming them street smart and envisioning they hold the pulse of New York under their hoods. Having had truly frightening taxi adventures in cities like Athens, Naples or Calcutta, they assumed New York cabbies would be tame—aka avoid driving on sidewalks and actually watch the road—by comparison.

When it comes to how taxi drivers think of tourists, many have dollar signs on the mind.

OK, so maybe that's an exaggeration, but only sometimes. Sure, some drivers love to chat up tourists and give them driving tours of New York—not just for the trip, but because they see themselves as mini ambassadors for the city. But most drivers don't care who's in back, so long as they're decently clean and they tip.

Ultimately, after visiting New York, tourists go home and regale their friends with dramatic cab stories and tales of kitchen cupboard-sized hotel rooms and thirty-five-dollar hamburgers. To New Yorkers, these stories would barely register as a blip on the radar screen. Last time my Ohio cousin visited, we grabbed a cab home to Brooklyn after a late night. The driver made exceptional time as well as a Batmobile-esque lane change across a three-lane highway. My cousin wildly grabbed for her seat belt and my arm. I complimented the driver on his control while sliding around the back seat. I doubt he even blinked.

THE DEADHEAD CONNECTION

~

John Kaminski*, like many other cabbies in the 1970s, was a Deadhead. He has a photo of himself with long blonde hair, a red beard and a Grateful Dead T-shirt, sitting on the back of his taxi. Back then, when people got into his cab, they invariably said, "Let me guess—you're a musician, right?"

Wrong. But he loved music and worshipped the Grateful Dead. His parents forbid him from joining the throng at Woodstock—he was only fourteen but it killed him that this incredible party was mere miles from the bungalow colony where he lived that summer.

He experienced his first Dead show at the Nassau Coliseum.

"It pretty much amazed me," he said. "They had a crystal ball and they were playing a slow song and we were kind of swaying. Then this guy behind me fell straight forward. He seemed to be alright. It was a different time back then."

A third-generation New York cabbie, John was months from launching his life as a driver when he met his wife in 1974. For their first date, he took her to a Dead show. One week later, they moved into a Bronx apartment together. They married three years down the road, and the following summer rented an RV and followed the Dead around New York for six weeks. It was a romantic honeymoon, and they gladly shared their motorhome bathroom with teenage Deadheads.

John was short of cash one night in the 1970s when The Dead played at Madison Square Garden. Otherwise he would have sprung for a ticket. Instead, he settled for parking his cab near the venue and watching Deadheads pile into the nearby Pennsylvania Hotel across the street. John was standing near his taxi when a Dead fan with a clean-shaven face and long, curly hair approached him.

"Hey man, where can I find a good tour of Manhattan?" the guy asked.

"Take a tour of the city!" he said. "I could show you the city inside and out! Get in the front seat."

Off they went.

"I've always been the man to take the tourists around," he said. "I was wild and crazy, a talker and a flirter. And I considered myself an ambassador to New York City. I loved picking up first-time tourists. I would talk all the way from the airports, unlike today when so many guys are on cell phones. Meeting people was the number-one fringe benefit of driving a cab. A prerequisite to life should be six months of driving a New York City taxi. You learn so much. No other place in the world is like this."

They talked while John drove. The passenger's name was Michael, and he flew in from California for the show. The summer day was hot and John's cab had no air conditioning, so they drove with the windows open, arms resting on the windowsills. They smoked some herb.

John took Michael through Chinatown and Little Italy. It was one of his favorite neighborhoods to show off. Canal Street, decorated in green, red and white, looked as Italian as Spumoni, while the other side, with it's Chinese symbols and dead chickens in the windows, clearly wasn't. They drove through SoHo, where litter blew through streets in front of the old warehouses. The Meatpacking District was just that—row upon row of meat distributors, whose garbage bags piled on the sides of the hot streets leaked blood. They made their way north towards Chelsea, where warehouses with broken windows rose up against the Hudson River.

"This is fantastic," Michael said, taking it in.

"Oh yeah," agreed John, who was having a great time explaining New York and watching the enraptured expression on Michael's face.

For his grand finale, John drove over the Brooklyn Bridge. The bridge's thousands of steel rivets made a ping-ping noise as the taxi crossed the East River. Michael looked to his right.

"Wow," he said, seeing the Statue of Liberty in the harbor.

Driving over the bridge on the way back to Manhattan, Michael got a full-on view of the city's skyline.

They cruised around for an hour before getting back to Madison Square Garden. John put the car in park by the hotel.

"How much do I owe you?" Michael asked.

"Nothing," John said. "Man, I gotta tell you, this was as much fun for me as it was for you."

"No, no," Michael insisted.

He reached into his wallet and pulled out a wad of cash, counted out three hundred dollars, and gave it to John.

John gawked at him.

"Are you sure?" he asked, not wanting to take it. "You don't have to do this, this is nuts."

"Take it man, I have a lot of money," came his reply.

"Okay," said John. He pocketed the cash.

A couple of years later, John met up with his old friend from Stuyvesant High School. His friend, a fellow Deadhead, had moved out to Lake Tahoe for his work as a geologist. They would talk on the phone occasionally, always comparing notes on Dead shows. This was one of his annual visits to Manhattan.

"Hey, I met a friend of yours at a Dead show," his friend said. "His name was Michael."

"Michael who?" John asked.

His friend said the last name. "I don't know who that is," John said.

"Yes you do," his friend said. "I was at a Dead show, and Michael was standing next to me. I was talking to him about New York, and he was telling me about this great cab ride he had. He said the driver shared a joint with him while giving him a tour of Manhattan before a Dead show at Madison Square Garden. At that point, I told him I had a friend who drove a cab. I told him your name and described you, and the guy recognized you right away. 'That's the guy!' he said."

John realized it was the Deadhead he befriended that summer day.

"You gotta be kidding me," he said.

"You know how they say it's a small world?" John said, looking back. "My mind was blown. I always wanted to catch up with that guy somehow. See what he was up to."

HAPPY THANKSGIVING

~

The bus stopped when it reached Manhattan, and Ned Braunschweiger got off and walked to a nearby row of taxis. It was Thanksgiving Day in 1969. Snow fell lightly and the roads were slick.

"Where you going?" the cab driver at the front of the line asked him. The cabbie stood beside his taxi, wire-rimmed glasses perched on his nose. A lightweight coat, a flimsy barrier against the winter cold, hung from his thin frame.

"The Commodore Hotel," said Ned, who was as wiry as the cabbie, although much younger at age thirty-two.

"Get in." The driver nodded to the cab.

Ned took a breath and got in the backseat. An older man with gray hair already sat in the front. Ned had never been in a yellow cab before. It seemed just like any other car. He leaned back in the seat. Today had been a day of firsts for him. It was his first flight—his stomach had dropped during while taking off and landing. He also couldn't remember the last time he took a bus.

Not least, it was also his first time in New York City. He made the trip for work, and while he had scoured books and articles on New York, he had no idea what to expect. The stress of all the 'firsts' made his stomach feel queasy. He just hoped everything would work out, and that he'd meet some nice people.

Ned looked out the window. One thing he did know: he hated crowds. Mobs of people made him anxious. He couldn't keep his eye on people, and he never knew what some stranger standing near him would do. Whenever he felt trapped in a crowd, his idea of paradise suddenly became standing alone in the middle of a cornfield. He loathed throngs so much that he turned down his dream job editing an industrial recreation magazine in Chicago. He refused to spend his days commuting on a crowded elevated train, only to squeeze himself into a packed elevator to reach his skyscraper office. His dream job didn't include the daily challenges of life in the city.

Instead, he settled on a job in his hometown of Toledo, Ohio, working in advertising for the Fortune 500 company, Toledo Scale. His bosses appreciated his quick wit and sharp eye for detail, and he appreciated the fact that his offices were inside a one-story plant stretched across former farmland.

The older man sitting in the cab's front seat turned around. "Where are you from?" he asked.

"I'm from Toledo."

"Oh, I'm from Akron!" he said.

The older man told Ned he worked with Ohio Edison. In turn, Ned shared with the man that Toledo Scale sent him to New York to set up a booth for the upcoming chemical convention and trade show.

A commotion of screaming erupted outside the cab, and Ned and the Ohioan stopped talking and listened. Ned looked out the window and saw their cab driver in a yelling match with a man wearing a heavy, expensive overcoat. Both men gesticulated wildly.

Ned looked at the man from Akron. They both shrugged. In that moment, they heard a 'thunk' as something was thrown into the trunk. The shouting continued and the trunk's hood was slammed shut, hard. The whole cab shuddered. In a huff, the driver got in the front seat, and the well-dressed man—the one arguing with the driver—got in the back of the cab with Ned.

The driver wrenched the cab into gear, while the third man grumbled insults at the cab driver under his breath. Ned couldn't make out his words, nor did he really care to. The cab driver ignored the muttering. Ned figured the man was drunk—who else would scream at a cab driver, yet still get in the cab, then mutter endlessly under his breath? As much as Ned hated crowds, he loathed drunks more. Not that Ned didn't have a weakness for brandy and beer, but true drunks meant bad news. He'd seen enough of them in action. They could laugh with you one minute and punch you in the face the next. Ned turned away from the man.

He adjusted himself in the seat. He hadn't expected anything bad to happen in New York, but overall, he had hoped for something better than this—being trapped in a cab sitting inches away from an angry drunk who was spewing a steady stream of abuse from his mouth. Ned tried to block him out. His mood sank lower and his acidy stomach felt even worse when he thought about his family enjoying Thanksgiving without him. His mother rarely cooked, but she could whip up a good dinner when she put effort behind it. He wouldn't get to see his niece

From Yellow to Green

~

Move over, Crown Victoria, here comes the Prius. New York's yellow cabs became a tinge greener as taxicab fleet owners began exercising their new-found right to buy hybrid cars, thanks to the "Clean Air Taxi Act." And not a moment too soon. New Yorkers don't need to see the results of official-looking surveys to know their air quality is among the worst in the nation. Anyone walking under an overpass for the crowded Brooklyn-Queens Expressway can practically smell the cancer in the air.

Although Mayor Bloomberg lost the battle when it came to having a fully hybrid fleet by 2012, he's still greening the taxi industry. As of May, fleet owners can charge drivers more to drive hybrids or clean diesel cabs. Owners will be forced to charge cabbies less to lease gas guzzlers, like the favored Crown Victoria.

In other words, becoming eco-friendly will make fleet owners richer.

New York taxicabs serve as the ideal vehicles to go green, as the difference in emissions between hybrids and traditional cars is most striking when city traffic slows to a crawl or when autos idle.

Even drivers get something out of the deal. Hybrids use less gas that cabbies pay for, meaning extra money may line drivers' pockets. In the long run, though, the hybrids' durability needs to be tested, making sure they can withstand the 100,000 miles annually put on most cabs. Currently, just over 2,000 taxis are hybrids.

Sherri race around on her little legs. Thanksgiving was a time for family, and he missed them.

The cab headed toward its first destination as the sun set. Traffic was light and the cabbie drove quickly, cutting in and out of cars. The taxi slid and fishtailed as the car ran across the partially paved-over metal streetcar tracks that ran along the slick road. The man in the pricey coat continued muttering and the driver continued ignoring him. But Ned could feel anger emanating from the driver, and assumed the man was taking his frustration out on the road.

Venting anger while driving was something Ned understood. He could hardly drive for two blocks without working himself into a seething lather at the ineptitude of other drivers and swearing loudly at the idiots on the road. For him, it was a healthy habit. Releasing his anger helped control the stomach problems that had lead to his medical discharge from the Navy. But his rage never stopped him from driving skillfully albeit aggressively; he had never gotten in an accident, and had avoided many because of his quick reflexes. One summer during college he even picked up shifts driving vans as a traveling salesman. Unlike the cabbie, Ned knew to respect the power of bad weather and black ice while driving. He just wished the cabbie would slow down. Ned had no intention of suggesting the driver take more care, but the taxi's sliding only made his churning stomach worse.

Ned exchanged a nervous glance with the man from Akron.

The driver turned onto Central Park South, and the cab skidded to a stop. The driver got out and slammed his door shut. The well-dressed man did the same. Within seconds the two started hurling curses and screaming insults at each other. The rich man shouted while standing on the sidewalk, and the cabbie responded while walking towards the trunk.

Turning around in the cab, the man from Akron addressed Ned. "This is a pretty ritzy district," he said. "That's Central Park over there."

Ned couldn't see the park through the darkness, nor could he make out the buildings' architecture. For as much as he tried to block out the fighting, it was all he heard.

From the corner of his eye, Ned saw a heavy suitcase fly through the air. It came out of nowhere and hurtled towards the well-dressed man. The suitcase hit the man in his gut, momentarily stemming his verbal assault and knocking him backwards a number of steps. He managed to catch it, then swore loudly.

The cabbie, who threw the suitcase, shouted back. He banged down the trunk and got back into the front seat. "Oh Jesus," Ned thought. He could see tension grip the driver, and didn't want to think about what would happen next. He braced himself as the driver reached over and hit the little flag on the meter, turning it off. He turned and looked at both men. "How are you gentlemen?" he asked in a pleasant tone.

"Fine," Ned and the other man answered. Ned waited for the explosion.

"I'm sorry you had to see that," the driver continued. "I should have been satisfied with two fares and should not have squeezed in a third." He paused. "Would you like to see the Christmas lights?"

"Yes, please," said Ned, taken aback by the change in events, and amazed at how quickly the cabbie seemed to have calmed down.

"Sure," the man from Akron echoed.

The meter off, the driver made his way onto Park Avenue.

The entire street glowed with Christmas lights. Ned took in the buildings, each decorated differently, some with glittering stars and some with long strands of white lights stretching stories high. He relaxed and smiled. Other buildings shone with the red and green designs running across their facades. Ned had never seen anything like it—skyscrapers glowing with candy-store colors, rows of lights draped from window to window, creating shapes and patterns that blended into a general impression of warmth and festivity when viewed from a moving cab. Little trees planted on a boulevard in the middle of Park Avenue sparkled with lights as it continued to lightly snow.

"I'm sorry I can't show you the Rockefeller Center lights, because they won't be up until tomorrow," the driver said.

He drove along, not too quickly, giving the Ohioans a guided tour of Midtown. He pointed out the different storefronts famous for their

Christmas displays. Ned and the man from Akron craned their necks to take it all in. Ned forgot about his stomachache. The driver told them about various landmark buildings, hotels, churches and civic buildings. The streets were nearly empty of cars, but Ned couldn't believe how the sidewalk teemed with people, some stopping to look at the merry displays, others hurrying by. He had never seen this many people about at night.

Both Ned and the man from Akron were staying at the Commodore Hotel, near Grand Central Station. When the driver reached the hotel, both men reached for their wallets although they knew the meter was off. The driver waved their money away, but both Ned and the other Ohioan insisted he accept a generous tip.

Full disclosure: Ned Braunschweiger is my dad. He still hates crowds, and he's a ranting maniac behind the wheel.

VERA WANG EXTRAVAGANZA

~

Kristin Jaskolka walked through Midtown, holding two shopping bags of recent clothing purchases. She spotted Leah, her brother's fiancé, standing at their designated meeting point. Kristin waved, and Leah smiled and walked towards her through a haze of afternoon drizzle.

"Hi! How'd the audition go?" Kristin asked.

"It went pretty well," Leah said.

Both she and her fiancé, Peter, were opera singers. They had traveled from Baltimore to visit Kristin and her husband.

"Are you ready to try on dresses?" Kristin asked, smiling.

"Oh yes," Leah said.

In anticipation of Leah and Peter's visit, Kristin made Leah a 4 p.m. appointment to check out wedding dresses at Vera Wang. Kristin, who worked as a marketer in the beauty industry, knew the best way to score a dress at the designer's upcoming sample sale was to sift through the sophisticated collection before the sale doors even opened.

The weather went from sprinkling to rain.

"Let's grab a cab," Kristin said.

She held her arm out, and a cab pulled over. They climbed in.

"We're going to Seventy-seventh and Madison," she told the driver.

The cabbie remained silent as he pulled away from the curb. His head almost touched the ceiling and his shoulders spanned the driver's seat. A hostile vibe emanated from the driver, but Kristin ignored it, smoothed down her long, blond hair and chatted with Leah about the wedding.

She offered to accompany Leah to the sample sale if she wanted. Kristin was a veteran at this. After all, she wore Vera Wang at her wedding. Kristin had researched her Vera Wang dream dress to the last stitch, and she and her mom arrived at the sale site at 5:30 a.m., hours before it opened. At least twenty giddy women with gigantic rocks on their left hands already waited in line, drinking coffee from thermoses.

Two massive bouncers stood by the door with their arms crossed.

When the time neared 8 a.m., the line stretched for blocks. The atmosphere was electric. The bouncer announced to the crowd that if any brides-to-be threw punches, yanked hair, or tripped anyone else, they would be physically removed from the premises. He had seen it before and wouldn't tolerate it.

Among the first women to dash through the doors, Kristin grabbed a couple dresses, tossed them to her mother and bolted to the dressing rooms. She ended up buying the first dress she tried on—at $1,150 it was a bargain, only one-quarter of its original price.

She just wanted Leah to have as beautiful a dress as she had.

Within a few minutes, the cab came to a stop. Kristin looked around and saw only scaffolding.

"We're going to Vera Wang," she asked the driver, knowing that cabbies often have exceptional knowledge of the city. "Do you know where the store is?"

"We're here lady," he said in a short, angry tone.

Kristin sensed he wanted them out of the cab immediately. No skin off her back. They paid, she got a receipt, and left.

The women found the store and checked in with the woman behind the counter. They were fifteen minutes early for their appointment, and the woman motioned to a leather sofa by the window. The two sat down and began flipping through wedding books.

Kristin's phone rang. It was Peter, her brother and Leah's fiancé.

"Where's Leah?" he asked agitatedly.

"She's sitting right next to me," Kristin answered.

She hoped her tone implied Peter should stop worrying. Yes, Leah grew up in Tennessee, but she could take care of herself.

"What's the matter?"

"Why is some strange guy answering her phone?" Peter asked.

"What do you mean?"

Kristin turned to Leah.

"Look for your phone," she said.

Leah dug through her purse but couldn't find her cell phone.

219

"I must have lost it in the cab," Leah said. "I think I had it in my pocket. It must have fallen out when I sat down."

The hunt was on.

Kristin called Leah's phone a number of times, but no one answered. Between calls to Leah's cell phone, she called her brother, keeping him updated. Kristin felt bad. Leah and Peter were essentially starving artists, and were saving for their wedding. Leah had just bought the phone. As the business-minded sibling, Kristin wanted to help them out. She wanted to get them the phone back.

Finally, someone answered Leah's phone.

"Hello."

Kristin recognized the cab driver's deep voice and handed the phone to Leah.

License to Drive

~

Outside of chutzpah and quick reflexes, anyone who wants to legally drive a cab needs a New York State chauffeur's license and a license from the TLC, lovingly referred to as a hack license. (Those wanting to illegally drive a cab need a crowbar, wiring skills and a look-out).

While most people can get their hands on a chauffeur's license, obtaining a hack license requires more effort. First, potential cabbies need to get fingerprinted, pass a physical and pass a drug test. Anyone who pees stems and seeds or has a past conviction can forget their dream of sitting behind the wheel. The TLC also requires a defensive driving course.

Then comes classroom time. Wanna-be drivers can either spend eighty hours in class, or choose the less time-consuming twenty-four-hour class, called E-Z License, a frightening name for a frightening concept. After all the preparation, applicants need to take the TLC's test and an English-language test—yes, even native speakers. Just in case.

"Hi, thanks for finding my phone," Leah said. "I was wondering if you could bring it back to me?"

Leah went silent, listening. Her brow furrowed in confusion.

"I don't understand what he's saying," she whispered to Kristin.

"Give it to me," Kristin whispered back, reaching for the phone.

She had a hard time making out what he wanted—his Caribbean accent thickened over the phone—but she finally realized that he was asking for forty dollars in exchange for the phone.

"Listen, I'll pay your fare," Kristin said. "You can't be that far, you dropped us off five minutes ago."

"I've got a fare," the driver said. "I have to hang up."

Click.

He called her back a few minutes later. Kristin tried to make out what he was saying, squinting her eyes to concentrate harder. All she understood was, "Lady, blah blah blah Bronx."

"Can you repeat that please?" she asked.

He did, angrily. She finally figured out that he told her she could pick up the phone from his dispatcher in the Bronx once his shift was done. Kristin had no intention of taking the hour-long subway ride to the Bronx.

"You can't be that far," she said. "How far away are you?"

"I've got a fare," the driver said, hanging up again.

The receptionist behind the desk at Vera Wang had been listening in.

"My God, I can't believe that!" she said. "That is not right."

Three young Long Island landscapers in baggy jeans, setting up a Christmas tree in the display window, also overheard.

"That sucks, man," one said.

"Only in New York," another chimed in.

"I'm going to call 311," Kristin said, dialing New York City's number for non-emergency problems.

She got the cab's receipt out of her wallet. She hoped 311 could trace the cab through the medallion number on the receipt.

"Hello, 311," a voice on the other end of the line said.

Kristin explained the situation with the taxi cab and the missing cell phone.

"This is a 911 issue," the respondent said. "I'll transfer you."

"Wait!" Kristin said. "Are you sure this is for 911? This isn't an emergency."

"Yes, I'm sure," she said, and transferred Kristin.

Kristin was not at all sure about speaking with 911, but the line was already ringing. She felt guilty that Leah was even in this situation. It seemed that every time Leah and Peter visited Kristin and her husband, something went wrong. The last time, they got both a parking ticket and a boot on their car. Kristin wanted Leah and Peter to feel comfortable in New York.

A calm voice came on the line.

"911, what is your emergency?"

Kristin launched into the story, giving the operator the cab's medallion number. The operator traced the cab to its garage, and put Kristin on hold to call the garage's dispatcher, who would know the guy behind the wheel. After a few minutes of waiting, the operator came back on the line, gave Kristin the dispatcher's number, and told her to call him.

She had just hung up when her phone rang.

"Hello?" she said.

It was the driver. Once again, she couldn't understand what he was saying; all she could make out was that he wanted forty dollars.

"OK, come to Madison and Seventy-sixth Street and I'll give you forty dollars for the phone," she said.

She had no intention of giving him forty dollars, not when the fare couldn't be more than fourteen dollars or so.

"I'll call you when I get there," the driver said.

After the driver hung up, Kristin called his dispatcher and told him the situation. "He really scares me," Kristin said, wrapping up the tale.

"I'm really sorry," said the dispatcher in a sympathetic voice.

He started to speak with her about what to do, but his other line beeped in. He put her on hold to take the call. He got back on the line.

"I'm so sorry, but I have to go, one of my drivers has gotten in a bad accident," he said. "Call me back, call me back."

"Okay," Kristin said.

She hung up, and Leah was called in for her appointment. Kristin opted to stay in the waiting room and wait for the driver's call.

Her phone rang. She picked up and heard the now familiar gruff voice, "I'm on my way, come out and meet me."

Kristin went outside. She didn't see the cab, but spotted a cop car on the corner waiting for a light. She hurried over and knocked on the window.

"Can you help me?"

"What's going on?" the cop in the driver's seat asked.

Kristin explained the situation again.

"Can you hang out with me here?"

"Well, is it your phone he has?" the cop asked.

"It's not my phone."

"Then I can't help you," he answered.

"The phone's owner is just in Vera Wang," said Kristin, looking at his female partner. "She can't come down."

"Well, I can understand that," the female cop empathized.

"Do you live in New York?" the other cop asked.

"No, I live in Hoboken," Kristin confessed.

"Well that doesn't help me!" the cop said.

"Can't you just hang out with me until he comes?" Kristin asked. "I'm scared of this guy. He's gruff and mean."

"Lady you watch too much Law and Order," the female cop said. "When he comes, just call 911."

They drove away. Kristin sighed and steeled her nerves. At least the landscapers in Vera Wang knew what was going on. She figured she could call them for help, if she needed to.

Her phone rang for what felt like the millionth time that day.

"Hello."

"I'm here," the cabbie said.

Kristin hadn't seen him because he had parked behind a parked car.

She walked over to the cab. His passenger window was rolled down. She was determined not to show him she was afraid.

"Give me the money," he demanded.

"Give me the phone," she countered in a steely, firm voice she reserved for people who annoyed her. "I don't have that much money."

"I drove all the way back here from Thirty-fourth Street!" he yelled.

"Thirty-fourth Street?" Kristin echoed.

She felt anxious, but refused to back down.

"That's a seven dollars for maybe a ten-dollar fare. I'll give you double that."

"No! Give me forty."

"I don't have forty dollars. I'll even let you look in my wallet!"

"I'm not going to do that," he said.

"What are you going to do, sell my phone?" Kristin pushed.

She needed that phone back, but was careful not to make him so mad he'd get out of the cab.

"Who do you think I am, lady, I have my own phone!" he screamed. "If I came out of my way to come here, I should get the extra money!"

"No you shouldn't!"

He glared at her, eyes narrow. "You can go pick it up in the Bronx then."

She couldn't believe his audacity. She was pissed.

"I'm standing here right now, you can give it to me right now," she yelled back. "Don't you have any human decency?"

The sparring continued. It was reaching a point that made Kristin nervous. She had no idea who this guy was, or what he was capable of. She wondered if he would hit her. Kristin's cell was in her hand. She held her phone discreetly below the window where the driver couldn't see it and called 911. She had the volume way up and heard the operator answer the line.

"Is this Kristin?" the operator asked, recognizing the number from Kristin's previous conversation with 911.

"Yes, this is Kristin," she said loudly and slowly, looking at the driver. "Why did you come here to the corner of Seventy-seventh and Madison? Did you come here to harass me? You're holding my phone for ransom!"

The cab driver looked confused; Kristin hoped the cops would pick up on her tips. She really hoped the cabbie wouldn't realize she called the police.

"Is he there now?" the woman on the line asked.

"Sir, you're scaring me!" Kristin said loudly.

"We're sending a car right now," the operator said.

Kristin kept arguing with the driver. Finally, he reached his limit.

"I don't need your stupid phone," he yelled, throwing it onto the street.

Kristin picked it up, and handed him ten dollars.

"I don't want your money, lady!" he shouted, throwing it back at her.

He peeled out of the parking spot. Kristin—the phone in her hand—walked back into Vera Wang.

The receptionist looked up.

"Did you get the phone back?"

Kristin smiled and held it up. She went up to the posh dressing room. Leah stood on the podium in front of the mirror, wearing a sleek white dress.

"My phone!" Leah yelled, hugging Kristin.

"What a good friend she is," said the woman helping Leah into the dress.

Nearly two hours later, when Kristin and her husband were driving to her father's surprise birthday party in northern New Jersey, Kristin got a call from the cops.

"Did you order this car from dispatch?" the cop asked. "Where are you?"

"I needed you over an hour ago!" she said. "Really helpful."

THE TIP

~

As a law student and a summer associate internship at a big-name New York firm, Paulette Schoenenberger* had two main responsibilities. First, to do legal research and write memos. And second, to attend a plethora of lavish recruiting events, like lunch at the exclusive restaurant Nobu or golf outings at West Chester country clubs.

That particular evening's events started with a wine tasting. Paulette couldn't bear to spit out all the delicious wines, so she finished a glass of every variety she tried. At the tasting she won a bottle of wine, which she and two other summer associates unceremoniously polished off while in one of the firm's offices.

By 11 p.m., Paulette was solidly drunk as she and two other summer associates headed to a party at a Midtown restaurant. The evening was wrapping up as they tottered through the door on their heels. Spotting the new arrivals, the lone remaining partner plunked down his credit card on the bar and began buying drinks. Paulette slammed back a few shots. She hazily noted they were bourbon, appropriate for a law student from the University of Virginia.

Paulette was vaguely aware of leaving the restaurant and the partner putting her in a cab. The driver took her to her Upper West Side apartment on Seventy-ninth Street. She stumbled out of the cab, across the street and into her building, greeting the doorman on the way in. She took the elevator to her floor and reached her apartment door before realizing that she didn't have her keys.

She didn't have her keys because she didn't have her two-gallon Louis Vuitton purse. Admittedly, it wasn't a real Louis Vuitton bag, but it was an excellent knockoff. She bought it in Shanghai for a few bucks as a joke, but the bag's quality stitching fooled everybody at her lawyerly events and made her look like someone with expensive taste.

"Shit," she mumbled under her breath.

She went back to the elevator, down to the lobby, and went to find the doorman.

"Is my cab driver still here?" she slurred. "I think I left my purse in the cab."

"Sorry, he's gone," the doorman answered.

Paulette was too drunk to worry about her purse. She just wanted to get into her apartment and pass out. So the doorman gave her the spare key, she went back up the elevator, into her apartment, and collapsed into bed.

The next morning, Paulette woke up feeling like a truck ran over her head. She felt even worse when she recalled that she lost her purse. She groaned out loud remembering what she had stashed in that massive bag—her wallet, cell phone, iPod and her company BlackBerry. She also had one hundred dollars in cash in her wallet.

Despite her hazy thinking skills, she computed the value of the lost loot in her mind, and the total came to about $1,500. But she knew almost nobody would recognize that purse as a knockoff—it looked like an $800 bag, bringing the value of the haul up to $2,300.

Every expensive item in the universe that she owned was in that bag. She groaned again and rolled over in bed.

"Oh, the shame of having to tell my law firm that I lost the company BlackBerry!" she thought.

Paulette wasn't clear on the details of how she got out of the taxi, but she couldn't imagine that the cabbie would have let her go without paying. She must have taken her wallet from her purse, paid the driver, put the wallet back into her purse, and then left everything in the cab. What an idiot move.

She sighed into her pillow and thought about a toothbrush. It was highly unlikely that the driver could get her purse back to her, even if he found it before another passenger with sticky fingers did. Her drivers' license was from California, and her student ID had her Virginia address. There wasn't a single item in her purse that had her New York address on it.

She forced herself out of bed, took a long, hot shower and got ready for work. She brushed her teeth extra hard, hoping it would kill the horrible taste in her mouth. It didn't. Her stomach felt queasy. Her head hurt.

She complimented her own foresight as she gathered the extra cash stashed around the apartment. Without it, she couldn't even take a cab or the subway to work. God, she was pathetic. What was she going to do without her purse?

Paulette made her way downstairs.

"Ms. Schoenenberger," the doorman called out as she walked by his desk. "The cab driver came back last night. He wouldn't leave your purse with me, but he left his phone number."

Hope spread through her chest and she felt a little less ill. She might actually get her purse back! She hoped the BlackBerry would still be there.

"Thanks!" she said, as he handed her a piece of paper.

On the way to work, Paulette thought about how much energy the driver must have expended to track her down. He had to have driven all the way back to her neighborhood without a paying fare.

He wouldn't have known which building on that block she lived in, so he would have had to walk up the block, talking to doormen until he found the one that knew her. And then had to be willing to drive

Why Yellow?

~

It wasn't until 1968 that New York taxis went yellow. Until then, each cab company had its own color—some were green, some had red tops, and some were brown and white. The city's many-hued cabs even made it into F. Scott Fitzgerald's *The Great Gatsby*, when Tom Buchanan's girlfriend, Myrtle Wilson, let four cabs pass before choosing to ride in a "new one, lavender-colored with gray upholstery."

It was the proliferation of gypsy cabs taking passengers from established taxi companies that led the city council to rule that all cabs be colored yellow, standardizing their look and helping customers differentiate between the legal and illegal varieties.

back the next day. She was amazed at the effort he spent to find her.

She also wondered why the taxi driver didn't just leave the bag with the doorman. She lived in a nice building, after all. Maybe he wanted a tip.

She walked into her office building buoyed by the thought that she might get her purse back. Reality hit when security wouldn't let her through because her company identification card was in her purse. She felt like an idiot as she called up to the offices and had someone come pick her up. Her head hurt.

The minute she walked into her office, she called the cabbie.

"Come on, pick up, pick up," she thought.

He didn't. She left a message. Half an hour later she tried him again. No answer.

Despite feeling like someone dropped an anvil on her head, Paulette attempted some work between unanswered calls to the driver. More importantly, she spoke with the other summer associates. Much of the evening was a blank to her, and she desperately needed them to tell her what happened.

Although she had the impression she only spoke with the shot-buying partner for half an hour, her friends assured her they chatted for closer to two hours. She was horrified. What had she said to him? To a partner! This was so embarrassing. She didn't feel better when her friends jokingly called him Blackout Partner.

All summer long she had worked to impress people at the firm. She hated the fact that her effort could unravel in one drunken night. She prayed she hadn't told the partner anything incriminating. And losing the BlackBerry would be a black eye on her record. How could she be so irresponsible?

She called the cabbie again. No luck.

Despite having zero appetite, she went to lunch at the trendy Midtown restaurant Dona with five lawyers from the firm. She pulled herself together and tried to impress them, but when they ordered numerous bottles of wine and plates of trembling, raw seafood to share, Paulette almost vomited.

When she got back from lunch, her office phone rang. Hope surged through her and she leapt at it. It has to be the cabbie! It was Blackout Partner. He wanted to make sure she had gotten home alright. She assured him everything was fine, and thanked him for putting her in the cab. She neglected to tell him about the missing purse and BlackBerry.

The phone rang again. She picked it up. It was the cabbie! He had her bag, and would stop by during his shift, which started at 4 p.m.

Paulette left work early. She refused to miss the cabbie when he came by.

It was 7 p.m. when Paulette's doorman called up to her apartment and said the cabbie was there. She rushed downstairs. When she saw the driver, she couldn't even pretend to recognize him. She never noticed that he was Middle Eastern or that he looked slightly younger than her father. Oh, she had been so drunk! He smiled at her and handed her the massive purse. Then he grew stern.

"You need to be careful," he said.

Embarrassed by her drunken state the previous night, Paulette responded with a joke and a self-deprecating remark.

But the driver was not to be put off so easily.

"New York City can be dangerous," he said in his accented English. "When you are alone, you have to be careful. Do not be careless with your own safety," he insisted in a fatherly way.

"I know, thank you," she said, still embarrassed, but appreciating what he was trying to do.

But he wasn't done yet. He launched into a short lecture on drinking, living alone and being careful. Paulette listened, and when he was finished, she said "Thank you" and gave him forty dollars from her wallet. He accepted the money. Paulette and the cabbie said their good-byes, and he left.

Although he took the reward she offered, Paulette felt that wasn't why he came back. She was convinced that he wanted to speak with her, and urge her to take better care of herself.

When Paulette looked inside her purse, she saw everything was still there, from the one hundred dollars cash to the beat-up umbrella she carried around. "There were a number of times I left things in cabs—one time I left my passport—and I have never seen them again," she said.

"It was kind of amazing. He didn't touch a single thing. I was so thankful. And I deserved the lecture."

CEILITO LINDO

~

During the mid-1970s, David Pollack drove to the Waldorf Astoria, near Central Park, to pick up a fare. Four guys stood out front decked out in black, closely-fit clothing with gold and silver trim, sombreros, and boots. One guy had a guitar.

"They looked like they just got done serenading Chi-Chi's," he said.

They climbed into the cab, three in the back, including the guy with the guitar, and the fourth got into the passenger seat.

"Where to?" David asked them.

"JFK Airport," the guy up front said in a Spanish accent.

"Where you guys from?" David asked.

"España," he said.

The band had been flown in for one performance at the hotel and were headed back to Spain. David didn't stop to contemplate why Mariachi singers would live in Spain rather than Mexico—instead, he was busy figuring out how he could take advantage of the fact that he had four professional musicians in his car.

Barely older than twenty, David had only been driving for a couple of years. He played piano and trumpet, and knew if singers were flat or sharp. He loved every kind of music. In junior high, he had a teacher who grew up on Park Avenue who took him to his first opera at age twelve. Once married, he would go to both the ballet and Grateful Dead shows with his wife. In his cab, he listed to both classical and rock, although rock and roll was his favorite.

His grandparents used to own an old dump of a hotel in the Catskills favored by the area's top entertainers. He would hang out with them and the waiters, who were all seventeen or eighteen, just a few years older than him. He began digging doo-wop.

He also loved mariachi. "And oh, man, in the movies when you see the mariachis, when you hear the harmonies, with two or three people singing ...," he trailed off, reminiscing.

He saw the band in his cab as an opportunity.

"Tell you what," he said. "If you guys sing for me, I won't charge you for the ride to the airport. Just sing for me, and that will be that."

"What do you want to hear?" they asked.

He couldn't think of any mariachi songs except the time-worn standard *Cielito Lindo*, a Mexican love song so well known in the States that most Americans would recognize the chorus tune, *Ay, ay, ay, ay, canta y no llores* . . . (Ay, ay, ay, ay, sing and don't cry).

"Cielito Lindo," he said.

The men began singing the tune in four-part harmony while the man in the back seat accompanied them with his guitar. The car filled with sound.

They continued singing all the way to their terminal at Kennedy Airport, only Spanish lyrics and always in four-part harmony. They didn't use any sheet music. It was all by heart. David wished he had a tape recorder. "It was beautiful and crisp," David said.

David could usually zip to Kennedy Airport in forty minutes; sometimes thirty. But for this ride, he didn't go over the speed limit once. The sooner he got them there, the sooner the music would stop. He relaxed his posture, slinging his right arm across the passenger seat. "If someone had looked at me, my mouth was open, and I was smiling like crazy."

He got to the airport and pulled up to the terminal.

"Thanks a lot, guys, that was amazing," he said. "The ride is on me."

"Thank you," the guys replied. They gave him a twenty-dollar tip.

CHAPTER 9

LAST CALL

Closing Time High Jinks

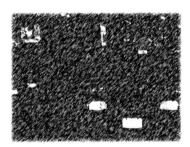

Cabbies give numerous reasons for working the night shift, often spanning the off-hour stretch from 4 p.m. to 4 a.m. Some drivers claim the night's happy drunks tip better. Others hate the endless daytime traffic jams that make hari-kari seem like a reasonable solution. Robert De Niro's character in *Taxi Driver* drove nights because of insomnia.

The city's energy changes at night. Confidence grows, heels and hemlines raise, lipstick darkens, and acquaintances pen adventures on the back of cocktail napkins. We feel creative, powerful, and sometimes, we feel drunk.

Late-night cab rides foster legends, despite the fact that not everyone remembers their ride home. Well, the cabbie remembers. It's hard for them to forget, what with that lingering vomit stench and all.

The stench makes me wonder about the advisability sitting on the cab's backseat. After all, a miniskirt leaves plenty of skin exposed to vinyl. Once, I watched an Oprah has an episode where Dr. Philip Tierno, head of New York University's microbiology department, swabbed people's homes from kitchen sink to toilet, telling them what kind of life-threatening funk grew there. Judging by the way he reacted to bacteria in a dirty sink, I figure he would recommend wearing a bubble suit before getting in a cab. Think about it. People have sex in cabs. They bleed, puke, cry, and pick their noses. The drunks pee in the backseat. Most of this happens after hours.

Filthy backseats don't prevent partiers from passing out in cabs. One driver had a loaded woman conk out with her skirt up around her waist. When his yelling didn't stir her—and because he was afraid of accusations—he found a cop to help him out. The male cop rapped at her windows. Nothing. Both were forced to stand around until she came to. (Note to the ladies—don't push this. The results of passing out in a cab can be much less pleasant, as certain woman will attest to.)

Another woman passed out in a cab, and groggily woke up having no idea where she was. She eventually realized she was in her old apartment—she had moved a few months previously. She pieced together that the cabbie must have looked at her drivers license, taken her to her old address, and somehow gotten her inside.

Just another challenge met by a driver embracing the adventure of driving nights. Or at least by a driver with breaking-and-entering skills.

THE SALSA-POWERED ACCELERATOR

~

Jason Gardner knew the schedule for trains from Manhattan to his folk's place in Westchester by heart. He also had discovered that getting on the MetroNorth at the 225th Street Marble Hill stop instead of at Grand Central bought him twenty additional minutes of drinking time with friends.

One Sunday, Jason knocked back a few and stayed at the bar later than he should have—specifically until 1 a.m. He was cutting it close, as the last train for the night left Marble Hill at 1:40 a.m. He jumped on the subway line to Marble Hill, but instead of making only express stops, the subway screeched to a halt at every single local station.

"No . . ." Jason groaned, as the subway crawled from Eighteenth to Twenty-third Street. Did the conductor go to sleep? At the next stop, Twenty-eighth Street, even the doors seemed to take their time opening and closing. He needed to get on that last train to Westchester. He had to make it. He had to get home. Jason looked repeatedly at his watch, willing time to slow down.

The subway didn't appear to move.

"Stand clear of the closing doors," a conductor mumbled into the intercom as the train inched forward again. God, they were barely at Thirty-fourth Street!

Jason looked at his watch again as signs for Forty-second Street slid by. The minutes ticked past.

He sat, tense. He could not miss that train. He had no friends in Manhattan to crash with. The friends he met at the bar lived in Hoboken; staying with them would mean a long trip back downtown, not to mention enduring New Jersey's painfully slow answer to New York subways, the Path.

"The next stop is Fifty-ninth Street." Jason could barely make out what the conductor said. The decrepit intercom system spat out the information as a garbled, incoherent mess.

Jason refused to even think about calling his parents, waking them up, and having them pick him up. He was an only child and they would do it, of course. But even the thought was embarrassing. He wasn't a teenager anymore. He may be living with his folks, but he had just graduated from Cornell. This housing arrangement would only last until he found a job.

The subway made its way into the next station. Jason glanced at his watch for what felt like the millionth time as they neared Seventy-second Street. It was 1:25. There was no way he was making it to Marble Hill on this train in fifteen minutes. He had seventeen more stops and 153 more blocks to go. Hell, they barely made it here from Fourteenth Street in the past twenty-five minutes.

He needed a new plan.

The subway doors opened. Jason ran out of the station and looked for a cab. There wasn't one. There had to be a cab! Finally, he saw one in the distance and hailed it. It was 1:30. He hoped he wasn't a lost cause.

He jumped in the cab. It was 1:31. He leaned towards the front.

"Listen, I've got nine minutes to make it to Marble Hill," he said, speaking to the cabbie in rapid clip. "Can you do it?"

"I'm from that neighborhood," the driver said in a Hispanic accent. "I'll do it in eight."

The cabbie peeled and the force of his acceleration pushed Jason backward in the seat.

"I'm screwed if I miss this train," Jason yelled up to the front. "I'll have to sleep in the streets!"

"Don't worry, man, I'm with you!" the driver said.

The driver changed the radio to a local salsa station and cranked the volume up all the way. The music's energy rushed through Jason and his eardrums felt close to bursting.

The driver floored it. The Sunday night streets were deserted. He peeled across town, and Jason slid drunkenly around the backseat. When the cabbie yanked his taxi right onto the West Side Highway, Jason put on his seat belt. The driver zoomed uptown while grooving to the salsa beat. Jason had never been in a cab that went so fast. In fact, he couldn't remember racing like this in any car. The driver seemed to have taken a personal stake in Jason making that train. All of the cabbie's energy focused on the road, and the music seemed to feed his speed.

"No problem," the driver called back to him over the Spanish-speaking singing. "I'll get you there on time. I'm from the neighborhood."

Jason didn't say a word.

The music blared as the driver banged back into the side streets at 220th before slamming on the brakes for a stop sign. He hammered the accelerator, screeched around a corner, and poured on more throttle on the way out.

This guy is crazy, Jason thought as he watched the scenery whiz by, everything a blur set to a Latin beat. He worried that the car might flip, but was too drunk to focus on that thought.

"How did I get into this?" he wondered. "This is how I could die!"

Despite the seat belt, he lunged forward as the cab braked for another stop sign.

It was clearly the driver's neighborhood. The man whipped through the streets the way homeowners can race through their over-furnished houses with all the lights turned off. For Jason, watching the driver was witnessing pure efficiency of motion.

Jason let the salsa engulf him, and a few minutes later the driver screeched to a halt at the Marble Hill station. From the cab, Jason could see the above-ground MetroNorth train a few blocks away. He looked at his watch. It was 1:38. The whole ride had only taken seven minutes, one minute less than the driver predicted. They had sped past 150 blocks. And this included slower side streets, turns, stop signs and red lights. Jason could hardly believe it.

He chucked him a twenty into the front seat, leaving a good tip, and ran towards the train, yelling, "Thanks man!" over his shoulder.

CABBIE CAVALRY

~

After a night of boozing, Adam Vargas* and his college buddy, Ben, decided to sop up the alcohol in their stomachs with a slice of pizza. Midtown is rife with pizza joints, so despite the early morning hour they found a place to buy a slice. The shop was crowded with the post-drinking crowd. They got in line.

In front of them, three drunk, loud guys in their early twenties were getting rowdy. Adam could tell they were from New Jersey because of their accents. They looked like part of the "bridge and tunnel" crowd, famous for bleached out jeans, gold chains, jelled up hair and meathead attitudes. A Brooklyn native, Adam recognized the signs.

They were all waiting to order when one of the kids looked at Adam and said, "Hey you big-nosed Jewish bastard!"

Adam turned to him, a look of disgust on his face.

"First off, I'm not Jewish," he said. "And second, you need to relax."

It wasn't the first time someone called him Jewish—not that he cared. But in reality, both his parents had emigrated from Colombia.

"Shut the fuck up, Jew!" the guy yelled, stepping closer.

Adam, a bit older and less jacked up than the guy, wasn't in the mood to deal with the idiot.

"Hey—you need to really watch what you're saying, especially in New York," he said, in a voice implying the guy ranked up there with toilet algae. He turned away.

But Adam's friend Ben didn't turn away. He stepped towards the drunk guys. With blond hair, blue eyes and standing at six-foot-one, Ben fit zero Jewish stereotypes, which explained why no one pegged him as Jewish. But he was. A Jew with a black belt in karate.

"What's your problem?" Ben said through terse lips, getting in their faces.

Adam is unclear on how it all started, but someone started pushing around someone else. Seconds later, both he and Ben were in a shoving match with the drunken Jersey boys. Their voices got louder, their pushes got more serious. The other customers moved away from them. Quick to react, the guys working behind the pizza counter rushed to the front of the store, and working in unison, forced all five of them out the front door and onto the sidewalk. Their shoving match continued on the street. The pizza shop employees pulled down the metal grate that covered the shop's glass windows and protected it from after-hour break-ins.

Someone threw the first punch and the groups paired off, with Adam taking on one guy and Ben another. Adam slugged his opponent in the face. The guy stumbled backward and fell. Adam spun around to separate Ben from his thug, when the third member of the Jersey crew jumped Adam from behind.

The guy twisted Adam around and held his arms behind his back, leaving Ben to fight the other two at once. Adam struggled to free his arms. Although his friend had valiantly landed some solid punches, he was taking the majority of the beating. Ben was forced back, step by step, punch by punch, towards a shop's display window.

With a fist landing on his jaw, Ben flew backwards into the window. The loud cracking sound sliced through the air. The glass shattered around Ben's body. He fell through the broken window. Shards of glass glittered in the air, then tumbled around him, bouncing off his body.

"Shit!" Adam yelled.

With a violent burst, he wrangled himself free and ran to his friend, who had dots of blood dripping from his face, arms, torso—it seemed like from everywhere. He forced his arm under Ben's shoulders and heaved him up.

"We'll get you a cab, we'll get you to the hospital," Adam told Ben. Ben didn't reply—his eyes were open, but his breath was quick and shallow. He had problems supporting himself.

As Adam helped Ben out of the window display, two of the guys ran at them. Adam hulled back and clocked one of the guys in the face as hard as he could, knocking him back. He bounced off the ground. His two buddies raced to his side, and Adam half-dragged Ben to the street, one arm around his friend, the other stretched out to hail a cab, easily the fastest way out of the mess.

A cab stopped right away, but when the cabbie saw Ben bleeding, he hesitated.

"What's going on?" he asked sharply, not letting them in the cab.

"Listen, I just need to take my friend to the hospital," Adam pleaded. "Can you please help us?"

The driver nodded. "Sure, get in the cab," he said.

Adam got Ben into the cab, climbed in after him and slammed the door shut. But before the cabbie could pull away from the curb, a fist slammed into the window closest to Adam. Adam propelled himself away from the window as the fist made contact with the glass again, harder. The window shattered, glass spilling onto the back seat and onto Adam. The guy attached to the first reached inside the cab with his head and arms, trying to grab Adam and Ben.

"Hey, listen, this is it!" Adam yelled, pushing at him. "This is squashed! Let's spend this! Get outta here!"

Half the guy's torso was in the car, his fists flying and his face contorted with rage.

"Look what you did to my friend!" the guy roared.

"Look what you did to my friend!" Adam said incredulously.

The cabbie, a small, middle-aged man, leapt out of the car, screaming in broken English. "What are you doing! You break my window! Get out of here!"

Just then, three other taxis pulled up behind Adam's cab. They were double-parked and slowed the flow off traffic. The drivers got out of their cabs. "What's going on?" they shouted, running towards their fellow driver.

"They broke my window!" the driver yelled.

The drivers turned towards where Adam's driver was pointing—at the three Jersey guys. The drivers started running towards them, and the thugs turned tail and ran down the street. The drivers chased them for half a block, at which time the police arrived on the scene and threw handcuffs on the Jersey boys.

The first people the police questioned were the cabbies, who motioned to Adam's driver. The police made sure Adam's cabbie was alright.

"Who's going to pay for my window?" he kept repeating.

The ambulance arrived and the paramedics lifted Ben into it. Adam rode to the hospital with him.

Adam couldn't believe what happened. The whole fight was so unexpected, and Ben falling through the window—that was just insane! But what he kept going back to was how three cabbies took over a huge chunk of Second Avenue and helped out their fellow driver. How they leapt from their cabs and, regardless of their own safety, chased after the guys. Adam guessed they took take care of their own.

TYLENOL BOTTLE TOILET

~

After a night of copious heroin and vodka consumption, Xanthe Adrastos* and Nadine left their friends at a hip Lower East Side bar and got in a cab. Nadine had to go to the bathroom, but she planned on holding it until they got home, typically a ten-minute ride. Their cab started heading towards Brooklyn, but within four blocks got stuck in a slow-moving traffic jam, something that rarely happens at 4 a.m., even in congested New York.

"I really need to pee," Nadine whined.

Xanthe glanced at her, eyebrow raised. The cab was heading onto the Williamsburg Bridge.

"I hope it's not a police checkpoint," she sighed.

The cops would sometimes stop all traffic on the Brooklyn side of the bridge, looking for drunk drivers.

"I need to pee so badly!" Nadine said, panicky.

A few minutes later: "I really need to get home."

The taxi crept on. The driver stared forward into the traffic, not reacting to any conversation he may have overheard. But they weren't even half way across the bridge when traffic came to a complete standstill.

"Fuck! What am I going to do!" Nadine exclaimed.

She sat slightly hunched over, like she was in physical pain.

They began to strategize, throwing out options.

"You could get out and go to the side of the bridge and squat down," said Xanthe, her mind hazy from the heroine she consumed, something she did almost all day, every day. "Or we could both go outside, and I could shield you with my jacket."

"No, it's too cold outside!" Nadine complained. "It's embarrassing. I don't want people to see me pee."

They continued to brainstorm solutions, but none worked for Nadine.

"Fuck it," Nadine said. "I have to urinate here."

She needed something to pee into, so they began fishing through their bags. Nadine pulled out a Tylenol bottle, about two-inches tall with an opening the size of her pinkie finger. She emptied out the last few pills.

"This will have to work," she said.

Xanthe started laughing into her hands.

Looking back, Xanthe can't remember if Nadine was wearing jeans or a skirt. What she does remember is Nadine, who was sitting behind the cabbie, turning around and kneeling on the seat, her back to the driver. She hung her butt past the seat's edge and over the seat well. She held the Tylenol bottle under her, as if she were collecting a urine specimen.

She started to pee.

Pretty much none of it made it into the bottle.

Xanthe watched, finding the situation horrifying yet hilarious, the fountain of urine splashing onto the floor. She was thankful for the one-inch-tall divider that separated her floor space from Nadine's, ensuring that Nadine's growing puddle stayed on her side.

The driver never turned around, never acknowledged what was happening. He stared straight ahead.

Nadine pulled herself back together and sat down in her seat. She and Xanthe laughed through the rest of the ride, but both were shocked that this had actually happened. That Nadine peed all over the floor. It seemed unreal—except for the smell. The smell was definitely real. The cabbie never reacted to the acrid scent, although he must have noticed it.

The taxi reached their building, and the cabbie wrenched the car to a hard stop by the curb.

"Get out," he said.

It would be his only acknowledgement that something had happened. They gave him money, he snatched it away. They bolted from the cab and raced up the stairs to their apartment, laughing.

Xanthe and Nadine re-told the story at parties hundreds of times. Their friends laughed hysterically, clutching their stomachs or emitting loud guffaws. It was fodder for hilarity.

"She's so crazy! She pissed in a cab!" they'd say.

The heroin she shot numbed the shame that bubbled up when Xanthe thought of the incident. Only after she checked into rehab and cleaned up did she deal with her real feelings.

"I was thinking, does the cab driver know this is happening? It was almost unbearable to me, the horror."

She was painfully aware of feeling class and race shame, of the cliché she fulfilled: that of a 20-something woman who played in a band, had serious substance abuse problems, and came from an upper-middle class or leisure-class background—Xanthe grew up attending exclusive private schools and lived in DC's Georgetown neighborhood with her lawyer father and journalist/teacher/homemaker mother. A techie, she frittered her generous salary away on drugs and rock 'n roll—"which was bullshit," she later said—went into credit card debt to fund her pricey heroine habit, and borrowed tons of money from her parents, lying about why she needed it.

The cab driver, who she guessed worked twelve-hour days, looked Middle Eastern, closer to fifty in age than forty. He spoke English with an accent. She imagined him coming to the United States to better his life, working hard, enduring grueling hours of mind-numbing labor, yet getting nowhere.

"The cabbie was so disgusted with us that it wasn't even worth yelling about," she said. "But I felt his quiet disgust. I also had the sense he'd seen that before. That he thought of his clientele as stupid, and that we belonged to this group."

A group born with advantages he never had; a group that abused their privilege.

She pictured the man cleaning up the urine, scrubbing the floor, scrubbing the seat, scouring the door. He would have to use bleach.

"It was his cab," she said. "He has to take care of it. It's kind of like pissing on someone's doorstep."

She realized that he probably wouldn't have been able to pick up any other fares after that ride, because of the smell. And if he paid one hundred dollars before his shift to drive the cab, he may have lost money on the day. But she didn't dwell on those things back in the day.

SNOW JOB

~

It was 2 a.m. on New Years Eve, and falling snow seemed to greet the first few hours of 1982. Lily Santiago and her three girlfriends—dressed in 1970s glam "pimp and ho" costumes of crazy ball gowns and anything glittery—stood at the corner of Second Avenue and Twelfth Street, trying to hail a taxi. They had just left the East Village joint where their friend bartended, and where they guzzled enough beer and cheap champagne to keep them decently warm. Still, they hugged their coats closely around themselves.

Lily was sick of holding out her arm while standing in snowdrifts. A native Brooklynite, she knew finding a taxi on New Years was nearly impossible, and the snowfall only upped the challenge.

Finally, they spotted an empty cab and hailed it. The driver pulled over, put the taxi in park, and got out. Lily noticed he was a little man. Without warning, he leaned over and puked into the snow.

"I'm too drunk," he slurred. "Someone else has to drive."

He turned around, opened the door to the back seat, crawled in, and passed out on the floor. The keys were still in the ignition.

The girls looked at each other.

"We got a cab!" yelled Maria, the wildest one of the group.

She jumped into the driver's seat, and turned the key. The car roared back to life. The other girls shrieked and clambered inside the car. Dewey called shotgun. Gail and Lily rushed into the back, careful not to kick the slumbering cabbie as they got in. Fortunately, he drove a large Checker cab, so they had plenty of leg room, even as he lay face down on the floor.

Only Dewey showed any hesitation. "Should we be doing this?" she asked.

"Hell yeah!" Lily answered. Although not as crazy as Maria, she had her moments. The daughter of Cuban and Dominican immigrants, Lily grew up in Brooklyn neighborhood reminiscent of *Saturday Night Fever,* but while she dug 1970s fashion, she shunned

248

the outer-borough disco scene for Manhattan's punk aesthetic. A hairdresser, she specialized in dreads, dye jobs and extensions ala Boy George, and even traveled to London to hone her craft.

Maria pushed on the gas pedal, and the cab skidded forward. Lily laughed as Maria plowed the taxi between the warehouses lining Chelsea's snowy streets. They made their way to the West Village. A few times Maria fishtailed as she braked at stop signs, but Lily didn't care. At least Maria could drive. She certainly couldn't—she was a New Yorker and could read a subway map; what did she need to drive for?

The driver looked up and groaned, flopping back down.

"That's creepy!" Lily said, raising her eyebrow and tucking her legs in closer.

They wound back to the East Village, passing the occasional groups of drunken revelers, although most people seemed to be inside.

AN AMERICAN ICON

~

One of the most recognizable taxis in history, the gas-guzzling yellow Checker cab has made its way through the 20th century's films and iconic photographs, becoming a symbol of urban life. Passengers considered the Checker the best of the cabs. Its monstrous bulk protected them from the outside world, the spacious backseat provided ample leg room, and the flip-down seats ensured that an entire family could rest comfortably.

Although supported by orders from New York, it was factory workers in Kalamazoo, Michigan who made Checker cabs. Run by Russian immigrant Morris Markin, the Checker Cab Manufacturing Company became the largest exclusive cab maker in the country by the mid-1920s. (Other cab makers also manufactured passenger cars.)

Later in the century, smaller, more fuel-efficient models won out over the two-ton Checker, and Checker Motors stopped cab production in 1982.

Lily couldn't believe how much fun this was. They laughed and cruised by when people standing on the street desperately tried to hail their cab. They never turned on the radio. It would have been too much stimulation.

Maria hulled through the Lower East Side. Somehow the snow on the street, or maybe the champagne bubbles in their brains, made everything look beautiful. At least the snow covered up the garbage and litter. Lights shining from windows sparkled on the vast whiteness. Many New Yorkers fearfully avoided these areas of Manhattan at night, but not Lily and her friends. They were local girls, through and through. They understood the city.

The clock ticked towards 4 a.m. The bars and clubs were about to close.

"Let's go look for people," Gail suggested.

The cab driver rolled over. Lily moved her feet out of the way.

Maria turned the cab, heading back to the East Village. They cruised by their favorite haunts, looking for friends. After a few drive-bys without recognizing any faces, they spotted a group of people they knew.

"Hey, you want a ride?" Maria yelled out the window.

"Maria! What the hell?" their friends said, laughing.

"Get in! We got a cab!" she shouted.

Their friends didn't need another invitation. The group of four nearly tumbled over one another in their attempts to reach the cab, all the while uttering exclamations of disbelief. The first friend to reach the door looked down as he climbed in the back. He paused, his foot still in the air.

"Who's that?" he said, motioning to the cabbie on the floor.

"Oh, that's just the driver," Lily laughed. "He sometimes picks his head up, mumbles something, then turns over, but he's down for the count."

"Wow," was all he could muster.

The spacious Checker cab, with its fold-down seats, had plenty of room, even with the driver lying at their feet. In no rush to drop anyone off, Maria cruised some more around Manhattan. There were nine people in the car, including the prostrate driver. The girls told their friends the story of how they got the taxi in the first place, and their friends shrieked with laughter, peppering the air with "No way!" and "No shit!" at appropriate moments. Then they dropped this pack of friends off, went back to the East Village, and looked for more people.

They picked up another group of friends and the scenario repeated itself.

The sun had started rising and the gas tank was low as Maria dropped off the rest of their friends. Lily and the girls considered filling up the taxi's gas tank, but decided against it. The last thing they needed was someone at the gas station looking into the cab, seeing the driver lying on the floor, and thinking they killed him.

As they all lived in Williamsburg, Maria drove the cab over the bridge to Brooklyn and drove up Metropolitan Avenue. They parked the car right outside Kellogg's, a twenty-four-hour diner coincidentally located across the street from where Lily would one day open her own salon, Lilypad. Lily and her friends chose the parking spot figuring the cabbie wouldn't be feeling too hot when he came to, and that he'd want a cup of coffee. They got out, locked the doors, and slammed them shut before splitting up and walking their individual ways home. Maria left the driver's keys on the front seat.

Acknowledgments

When I began this book, I was a straight-up journalist and needed plenty of guidance for my first foray into nonfiction writing. Thanks to Rebecca, Eli, Braxton, Kathy, Lee Bob, and especially Jeff, who went above and beyond in providing edits and feedback.

Unending appreciation goes out to the Paragraph crew for providing amazing support during the book's tougher moments.

I'd also like to thank Rita for being a tax goddess and Spencer for his web expertise; the Garden Grill for eggs and bacon, and Terry for joining us; Maumee Sarah for the long-distance calls, Missy (née Melissa) for s'mores; New York Sarah for my godson; Angie for Château Ghetto; Lori for meeting me at Dale's; and The Bagel Shop guys who continue to supply me with my daily carb overload.

Of course, I owe much to my extended family.

Thanks to Lee for believing in the book and sticking with it; Peter, of 671 Press, for joining the game; and the New York Taxi Workers Alliance for setting me up with some great cabbies.

And I'd especially like to thank all the taxi drivers and passengers who gave me their time and trusted me with their stories. You know who they are; their names are in the book.

LaVergne, TN USA
02 October 2009
159687LV00003B/102/P